The Baseball Entertainer

The BASEBALL Entertainer

EDITED BY

Robert Kuenster

Ivan R. Dee · Chicago

www.ivanrdee.com

Portions of this book first appeared in *Baseball Digest* magazine.

Library of Congress Control Number: 2008939783

ISBN-13: 978-1-56663-820-3 (paper)
ISBN-10: 1-56663-820-8 (paper)

PREFACE

Baseball, it's said, is the premier game of statistics. The numbers don't lie, as managers and fans can tell you. In no other team sport can individual accomplishments be measured so accurately as they can on the baseball diamond. The numbers give managers the rationale for their on-field strategies, determine annual awards, guide the trading and signing decisions of general managers, and serve as the meat for fans' debates. What are the most strikeouts in a game by a relief pitcher? Who are the only brothers to hit a home run in the same World Series game? Who are the five major leaguers with 3,500 or more career hits?

The Baseball Entertainer answers these and a lot more questions, some important, some trivial. And it tests your knowledge of America's pastime and the accomplishments of its great (and not so great) players. That's not all: If you think you know the rules of baseball, you'll be intrigued by the Rules Challenges that put you in the middle of confusing on-field situations—you make the call! You may never have seen it happen in a ball game, but there's a rule that covers it.

Photo quizzes and crossword puzzles round out the choice amusements in these pages, all designed for enjoyment.

If you're all ready then, let's play two!

The Baseball Entertainer

QUIZ 1

Answers on page 59

Here are quizzes to test your knowledge of baseball history and its players. Collect ten points for each question answered correctly. (If you score 80 or better, you are a Hall of Fame trivia buff; 70 or better, an MVP performer; 60 to 70, an All-Star; 40 to 60, a minor leaguer.)

1. Among the 27 players with 3,000 or more career hits, ten of them finished their careers with a batting average below .300. Collect one point for each of these ten players you can identify.

2. In 1966, Tim McCarver of the St. Louis Cardinals became the first catcher since 1900 to lead his league in triples. Who is the only other catcher to top his league in triples: Carlton Fisk, Ivan Rodriguez, John Wathan, or Craig Biggio?

3. Through 2008, there have been 22 pitchers who have won a World Series game for more than one team. Who is the only one of these hurlers to win a Fall Classic contest for three different clubs: Grover Alexander, Jack Morris, Nelson Briles, or Curt Schilling?

4. During his career, Reggie Jackson tied for the American League home run title three times — in 1975 with Oakland, 1980 with the Yankees, and 1982 with the Angels. In each of those years, the player who tied him for the league lead in homers was a member of the Milwaukee Brewers. Collect ten points if you can identify any one of the three Brewers players who tied Jackson for a home run crown.

5. Who is the only pitcher in major league history to win the Rookie of the Year, MVP, and the Cy Young Award: Vida Blue, Don Newcombe, Sandy Koufax, or Dwight Gooden?

6. Rickey Henderson is the career record holder for most runs scored with 2,295 — breaking Ty Cobb's mark of 2,246. Collect two points for each of the other five major league players you can identify who scored 2,000 or more runs besides Henderson and Cobb.

7. Which player (with a minimum of 5,000 career plate appearances) holds the highest career batting average without ever winning a league batting title: Riggs Stephenson, Joe Jackson, Albert Pujols, or Eddie Collins?

8. Eddie Murray holds the lowest career slugging percentage (.476) among sluggers with 500 lifetime home runs. Who is the only other player with 500 or more homers to finish his career with a slugging percentage below .500: Reggie Jackson, Ernie Banks, Rafael Palmeiro, or Mike Schmidt?

9. Who is the only player to total 2,000 or more hits, walks, runs, and RBIs during his career: Ted Williams, Ty Cobb, Barry Bonds, or Babe Ruth?

10. Who is the only player to achieve 100 or more extra-base hits in a season in consecutive years: Chuck Klein, Todd Helton, Lou Gehrig, or Hank Greenberg?

CROSSWORD PUZZLE 1

Answer on page 59

ACROSS

1 Dallas ____, who managed Phillies to 1980 World Series title

4 Leaving runners on base

9 Pete Rose was noted as one

10 David Ortiz's nickname

11 With the score tied in the top of the ninth, a grand slam by a visiting player often ____ (assures) a victory for his team

12 Hall of Famer Musial

13 Alex ____, an outfielder for the Toronto Blue Jays

15 Former managers Mauch, Michael, and Lamont

17 Slang term for third base

20 The ball ____ (bounced back) after hitting the outfield wall

22 Former Expo known as "Le Grande Orange"

24 Not out

25 A one-sided game

26 Whitey Ford was a ____ pitcher for the Yankees

29 Was behind in a game

30 Pitcher "Kid" ____ won 361 games

31 Casey Stengel was dubbed "The Old ____"

32 Charlie ____ played "Wild Thing" in the baseball comedy *Major League*

DOWN

1 Hall of Fame second baseman for the Tigers who was American League MVP in 1937

2 An AA minor league

3 Nonexistent, like the old Federal League

4 Took an extra base, _____ a double into a triple, or a single into a double

5 _____ Yount

6 A pitching coach often _____ a young hurler about the importance of not giving up walks

7 Heritage of Joe DiMaggio and Yogi Berra

8 The ways in which pitchers hold the ball

14 Easily retires a number of batters, _____ 'em down

16 A _____out means an opponent has failed to score a run during a game

18 Atlanta's ballpark is named after him

19 Nate _____, who has pitched for the Tigers

21 Warren Spahn was born in this upper New York State city

23 Managed the Astros, A's, and Mets

24 A pitcher will often _____ _____ (2 wds.) a batter to make him think a fastball is coming when it's really going to be a changeup

25 Doesn't play, _____ the bench

27 Former pitcher Vida _____

28 Top pitchers

QUIZ 2

Answers on page 61

1. Through the 2008 season there have been 23 players who have hit 30 or more home runs in their rookie year in the major leagues. Collect ten points if you can identify ten of these sluggers.

2. Identify the only two managers to win a World Series title in both the American and National League. Collect five points for each correct answer.

3. Which player holds the record for most 40-double seasons (ten) during his career: Pete Rose, Stan Musial, Tris Speaker, or Carl Yastrzemski?

4. The lowest total of extra-base hits for a batter with 200-plus safeties in a season is 25. Which player holds this mark: Maury Wills, Lloyd Waner, Ichiro Suzuki, or Rod Carew?

5. The most strikeouts in a game by a relief pitcher is 16, set by what hurler: Randy Johnson, Dick Radatz, Walter Johnson, Denny McLain, or Moe Drabowsky?

6. Since 1900, there have been only six players who have won a league batting title with two different teams. If you can identify any one of these players, collect ten points.

7. Who is the only major league player since 1900 to lead his league in hits for three different teams: Alex Rodriguez, Wade Boggs, Eddie Murray, or Paul Molitor?

8. Many players in major league history have hit home runs for seven or more clubs, but who holds the record for hitting a home run for 11 different big league teams: Bobby Bonds, Todd Zeile, Kenny Lofton, or Rickey Henderson?

9. A player totaling 40 or more doubles and 40 or more home runs in the same season has been accomplished several times in the majors, but who is the only slugger to belt 50 or more doubles and home runs in the same campaign? Babe Ruth, Hank Greenberg, David Ortiz, or Albert Belle?

10. Since 1969, when saves became an official statistic in the major leagues, only three pitchers have been credited with a complete game no-hitter and led their league in saves. Collect ten points if you can identify one of these pitchers.

12

RULES CHALLENGE 1

Answers on page 63

Following are ten True or False questions. If you get all ten correct in a given quiz, you are an expert on rules. A score of six to eight correct answers gives you a passing grade. Anything less indicates you need a course in Baseball Rules 101.

1. The San Francisco Giants have Fred Lewis on first and Aaron Rowand on third. The Colorado Rockies' infield is playing shallow to make a play at the plate. Randy Winn smashes a hot ground ball that goes between the legs of Colorado first baseman Todd Helton. The ball strikes Lewis advancing from first to second. The umpires correctly keep the ball alive and in play. True or False?

2. Evan Longoria of the Tampa Bay Rays hits a pop-up toward the first-base dugout. Kansas City Royals' first baseman Ross Gload and catcher John Buck converge to make the catch. Gload goes down into the dugout and catches the pop-up. This is a legal play and Longoria should be called out. True or False?

3. Carlos Quentin of the Chicago White Sox rips a line drive that strikes the third-base bag and deflects into the third-base dugout. This is a dead ball, and the umpires should give Quentin first base only since the ball never went beyond first or third base. True or False?

4. Aaron Miles of the Cardinals squares around to bunt. He gets the bat on the ball, but his left foot is partially on home plate when he lays the ball down the third-base line. The ball rolls foul. Miles should bat again since the ball rolled foul. True or False?

5. As Brandon Webb of the Diamondbacks delivers the pitch, a beach ball bounces into left field behind the fielder. Chicago Cubs' batter Derrek Lee rips a line drive into the alley in left center. Arizona left fielder Eric Byrnes scoops it up and throws it to second where Lee goes in standing.

Diamondbacks manager Bob Melvin argues that "time" should have been called and the play nullified. The umpires properly agree. In this case, Lee should bat again. True or False?

6. Justin Morneau rips a shot down the right-field foul line that looks like an apparent double. As the Minnesota Twins' first baseman rounds first, he stumbles and injures his leg. The first-base coach, Jerry White, grabs Morneau's hand and helps him get back to first. Since the coach did not push him toward the next base, Morneau should be allowed to stay at first base. True or False?

7. The Los Angeles Angels' Chone Figgins attempts a steal of second. He slides hard into the base and it comes out of the ground and lands several feet away. Seattle Mariners' second baseman Jose Lopez tags Figgins, who is not touching the base. Figgins should be called out. True or False?

8. There are two strikes on Hanley Ramirez of the Florida Marlins. He decides to surprise the defense and squares around to bunt. Washington Nationals' pitcher Jon Rauch is surprised and fires a wild pitch. Ramirez tries to avoid the pitch, but the ball hits his bat and rolls foul. Ramirez should not be called out since it was not his intention to bunt the wild pitch. This is simply a foul ball. True or False?

9. The Philadelphia Phillies' Cole Hamels has a no-hitter in the ninth with one out. With Carlos Beltran on first for the New York Mets, David Wright raps a ground ball between first and second. The ball strikes Beltran who is en route to second, preventing Chase Utley from making a play. Beltran should be called out and Wright should be credited with a hit, breaking up Hamels' no-hitter. True or False?

10. Derek Jeter of the New York Yankees hits a ground ball to Red Sox first baseman Kevin Youkilis. Boston pitcher Jon Lester comes over to take the toss from Youkilis, but contact occurs between Lester and Jeter while Lester is waiting to receive the ball from Youkilis. Obstruction should be called on Lester, and Jeter should be given first base. True or False?

14

QUIZ 3

Answers on page 64

1. Only four players have hit 200 or more career home runs in both the American and National League. Collect ten points if you can identify two of these four sluggers.

2. Who set the single-season mark for triples with 36 in 1912: Joe Jackson, Owen Wilson, Larry Doyle, or Kiki Cuyler?

3. Five players have had a 200-hit season in both leagues, including George Sisler (Browns/Braves), Al Oliver (Rangers/Expos), Bill Buckner (Cubs/Red Sox) and Vladimir Guerrero (Expos/Angels). Who is the only other player to accomplish this feat: Steve Sax, Bret Boone, Nomar Garciaparra, or Tommy Davis?

Ted Williams

4. Who is the only player to collect 1,000 or more hits in both the American and National League: Frank Robinson, Dave Winfield, John Olerud, or Bobby Bonds?

5. Nine pitchers have won both the Cy Young and MVP award in the same season. Collect ten points if you can identify five of these nine hurlers.

6. In 1942, Ted Williams won the Triple Crown, batting .356 with 36 home runs and 137 RBIs, but failed to win the American League MVP award. Which New York Yankee beat out Williams for the award: Joe DiMaggio, Phil Rizzuto, Joe Gordon, or Charlie Keller?

7. Who holds the major league record for most home runs hit in one month with 20: Sammy Sosa, Rudy York, Alex Rodriguez, or Barry Bonds?

8. Who was the youngest batter to collect 3,000 hits in the major leagues at the age of 34 years and 245 days: Robin Yount, Hank Aaron, Ty Cobb, or Pete Rose?

9. Only 19 players have recorded 200 or more hits while stealing as many as 50 bases in the same season. If you can identify five of these players, collect ten points.

10. Since 1900, 13 players have slugged four home runs in one big league game. Collect ten points if you can identify five of these 13 players. A clue: eight of these players did it for an American League team and five for an N.L. club.

PHOTO QUIZ 1 *Answers on page 66*

Here is a photo quiz to test your memory of who's who in baseball. Collect five points for each player you correctly identify. (If you score 80 or better, your memory is excellent; 70 or better, it's still good; 40 to 60, it's slipping.)

A   B   C   D   E

F   G   H   I   J

K   L   M   N   O

P   Q   R   S   T

1	Hank Aaron	15	Joe Jackson
2	Grover Alexander	16	Reggie Jackson
3	Johnny Bench	17	Chipper Jones
4	Yogi Berra	18	Bob Lemon
5	Vida Blue	19	Christy Mathewson
6	Larry Bowa	20	Pete Rose
7	Lew Burdette	21	Gary Sheffield
8	Ron Cey	22	Al Simmons
9	Don Drysdale	23	Reggie Smith
10	Bob Feller	24	Warren Spahn
11	Prince Fielder	25	Rick Sutcliffe
12	Hank Greenberg	26	Kerry Wood
13	Gil Hodges	27	Carl Yastrzemski
14	Carl Hubbell	28	Cy Young

Most Runs Batted in at the All-Star Break

A player has reached 90 or more RBIs by the All-Star break only 11 times since 1933, and only two players have exceeded 100 RBIs before the mid-season break.

Player, Team	Year	G	RBIs at break	Season total
Hank Greenberg, Tigers	1935	76	103	170
Juan Gonzalez, Rangers	1998	87	101	157
Carlos Delgado, Blue Jays	2003	94	97	145
Manny Ramirez, Indians	1999	78	96	165
Josh Hamilton, Rangers	2008	96	95	130
Harmon Killebrew, Twins	1969	96	91	145
Preston Wilson, Rockies	2003	95	91	141
Lou Gehrig, Yankees	1934	73	90	165
Tommy Davis, Dodgers	1962	89	90	153
Tony Perez, Reds	1970	88	90	129
George Foster, Reds	1977	89	90	149

QUIZ 4

Answers on page 66

1. In 1974, Joe Rudi, Sal Bando, and Reggie Jackson of the Oakland A's finished second, third, and fourth respectively in the American League MVP voting. Who was the 1974 MVP award winner in the A.L. who beat out the Oakland trio and led the league with 118 RBIs? Was he Carl Yastrzemski, Dick Allen, Jeff Burroughs, or George Scott?

Babe Ruth

2. Barry Bonds won consecutive MVP honors twice during his career, with the Pirates in 1992–1993 and the Giants in 2001–2004. Collect one point for each of the other ten players to win the MVP award in consecutive seasons.

3. Collect ten points if you can name three of the four players to club 500 or more career home runs and total 3,000-plus hits in the major leagues.

4. Which pitcher holds the record for most career shutouts with 110: Grover Alexander, Christy Mathewson, Cy Young, or Walter Johnson?

5. Among pitchers with 300 or more lifetime victories, which of these hurlers completed the fewest career shutouts with 25: Tom Glavine, Lefty Grove, Greg Maddux, or Tim Keefe?

6. Since 1969 when the save became an official statistic, only four relief pitchers have led the league in saves in both the A.L. and N.L. during their career. Collect ten points if you can identify two of these four closers.

7. Since 1900, who was the first player to steal 100 or more bases in a single major league season: Lou Brock, Maury Wills, Ty Cobb, or Rickey Henderson?

8. Between 1900 and 2008, only nine pitchers have had multiple 300-strikeout campaigns in the majors. Collect ten points if you can identify four of these nine fireballers.

9. Only seven players since 1900 have led their league in hits for three consecutive seasons, including Frank McCormick (1938–1940), Rogers Hornsby (1920–1922) and Ginger Beaumont (1902–1904) in the N.L. and Ty Cobb (1907–1909), Tony Oliva (1964–1966), and Ichiro Suzuki (2006–2008) in the A.L. Who was the only other player to accomplish this feat: Pete Rose, Wade Boggs, Kirby Puckett, or Tony Gwynn?

10. In 1924, Babe Ruth became the first of only two players — since strikeouts were first tabulated in the majors — to lead the league in strikeouts and batting average in the same season. Who is the only other player to win a batting title while pacing the league in strikeouts: Roberto Clemente, Jimmie Foxx, Dave Parker, or Stan Musial?

Name That Award Winner

A. This player is a two-time Most Valuable Player award recipient, hitting 500-plus home runs during his career. He won one league batting title. He never appeared in a World Series. He played as a freshman on Auburn University's football team. Who is he?

B. This pitcher won two Cy Young Awards despite winning only 131 career games in the majors. He was the first American League pitcher to win the MVP and Cy Young Awards in the same season. He was originally signed by the Chicago White Sox in 1962, starred for the Detroit Tigers, and his last club was the Atlanta Braves. Who is he?

C. This player and Carlton Fisk are the only catchers to win a Gold Glove and Rookie of the Year honors in the same season. He was the All-Star game MVP in 1997. He is one of only two catchers to put together a 30-game hitting streak in the majors. Who is he?

D. This player is a two-time World Series MVP winner. He won one league Most Valuable Player award. He stole 228 bases, drove in 1,702 runs, collected 2,584 hits, fanned 2,597 times, and clubbed 563 home runs. Who is he?

Answers on page 68

CROSSWORD PUZZLE 2

Answer on page 68

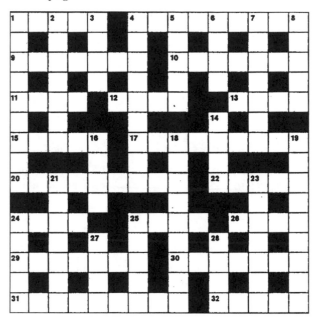

ACROSS

1 Four-bagger

4 White Sox outfielder 1968–1976, he then became a Yankee after a trade for Ken Brett

9 Fenway Park is home of "The Green ____"

10 Experienced ballplayer

11 Bobby Thomson was nicknamed "The Staten Island ____"

12 Buddy ____ was once skipper of the Royals

13 Willie Randolph managed this club in 2007

15 Pitcher Babe ____ won three World Series games for the Pirates in 1909

17 This surface was first used in Houston's ballpark

20 He played first base for the Cubs in 2008

22 An ____-innings game goes long

24 He played third base for the Cubs from 1932 to 1947, ____ Hack

25 "____ Papa" Bell

26 Former catcher for the Giants and White Sox, ____ Hill

29 State where teams have their spring training bases

30 Earlier in his career, Yankee owner George Steinbrenner was noted for his many managerial _____ (sackings)

31 Jeremy _____, a right-hander who has pitched for the Tigers

32 Martinez on the mound

DOWN

1 Series of games at a team's own park

2 The "_____ Line" is a batting average of about .215, the career mark of a former Pirates shorstop

3 Movie actor John Goodman played him in *The Babe*

4 This pitch has often been called an "Uncle Charlie"

5 The Red Sox have long been the Yankees' main _____

6 Teams are allowed three per half-inning

7 Justin _____ of the Twins was named the American League MVP in 2007

8 Abreu, Damon, and Cano were all _____ in 2008

14 David _____ was the A.L.'s Cy Young Award winner in 1994

16 Enter the batter's box, _____ up to the plate

18 Roughs up a pitcher (3 wds.)

19 The "Say Hey Kid" made his mark in New York and San _____

21 When Jim Thome comes to the plate, managers will often _____ (reposition) their infielders

23 Worked out

24 Rusty _____

25 Enchant

27 Space between two infielders, commonly the area between third and short

28 Field a line drive after a short hop

Uecker, a Team Player

Former big league catcher and current broadcaster for the Milwaukee Brewers Bob Uecker once was reviewing some of his career highlights with Johnny Carson on the *Tonight Show*.

Uecker: "I made a major contribution to the Cardinals' pennant drive in 1964 — I came down with hepatitis."

Carson: "How'd you catch it?"

Uecker: "The trainer injected me with it."

QUIZ 5 Answers on page 69

1. Excluding pitchers, there have been 135 Most Valuable Player award winners from 1931 through 2007. Among those MVPs, only 26 batted below .300 the year they captured the award. Which of those 26 posted the lowest batting average at .267: Roger Maris, Marty Marion, Harmon Killebrew, or Reggie Jackson?

2. Since 1947 when the Rookie of the Year award was first presented in the major leagues, five of its recipients went on the collect 3,000 or more career hits. Collect ten points if you can identify three of the five Rookie of the Year award winners who reached the 3,000-hit plateau.

3. Which one of the following pitchers won 20 or more games in his first major league season but did not capture his league's Rookie of the Year honors: Tom Browning, Herb Score, Dwight Gooden, or Rick Sutcliffe?

4. Which one of the following players holds the mark for most 200-hit seasons with ten: Stan Musial, Wade Boggs, Pete Rose, or Ty Cobb?

5. There are only five major league players with 3,500 or more career hits. Collect two points for each of these batters you can identify.

6. In the 1986 World Series, the Boston Red Sox were one pitch away from the title in Game 6 before a New York Mets batter eventually hit a ball that went through first baseman Bill Buckner's legs to allow the winning run to score from second base for the Mets. For five points, who was the Mets batter, and for five more points, who scored the winning run in New York's 6-5 victory?

7. Which manager has been credited with the most career victories (1,905) without winning a World Series title: Lou Piniella, Al Lopez, Gene Mauch, or Dusty Baker?

8. Alex Rodriguez is one of only two players in major league history to hit 40 or more homers in a season with three different teams. Who is the other player to accomplish this feat: Gary Sheffield, Jim Thome, Reggie Jackson, or Dick Allen?

9. Which player has the most career runs batted in (1,903) without ever leading his league in RBIs: Eddie Murray, Dave Winfield, Willie Mays, or Ty Cobb?

10. When Rod Carew collected his 3,000th career hit on August 4, 1985, which pitcher collected his 300th career win on the same date: Steve Carlton, Don Sutton, Gaylord Perry, or Tom Seaver?

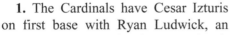

RULES CHALLENGE 2

Answers on page 70

1. The Cardinals have Cesar Izturis on first base with Ryan Ludwick, an improper batter, at the plate. Izturis advances to second on a Zach Duke wild pitch. Ludwick then raps a line drive to left scoring Izturis. The Pirates properly appeal the batting out of turn, claiming that Albert Pujols should be the proper batter. The umpire upholds the appeal. He should call Pujols out and allow Izturis to score. True or False?

2. In the above scenario, Pittsburgh Pirates' manager John Russell argues that Izturis should be returned to first base since he advanced on the bases while Ludwick, an improper batter, was at bat. The umps should return Izturis to first base. True or False?

3. With Carlos Lee on second base for the Astros, a wild pitch eludes Milwaukee catcher Jason Kendall. The ball bounces toward the backstop and near the Brewers' ball boy. Trying to get out of the way, he accidentally kicks the ball, and the runner takes an extra base to score. The umpire properly allows the play to stand. True or False?

4. Ian Kinsler is on first base for the Texas Rangers and running with the pitch when Josh Hamilton lines a shot to Tigers right fielder Magglio Ordonez. By the time Ordonez fires the ball back to first to double-up Kinsler, Ian is past second base. Ordonez's throw is wild, however, and goes into the first-base dugout. Since Kinsler had second made when Ordonez released the ball, the umps correctly rule that Kinsler should be allowed to score. True or False?

5. The Dodgers have runners on first and second when Manny Ramirez smashes a ground ball past Cubs shortstop Ryan Theriot. The ball hits umpire Bob Davidson, who is stationed behind the infielder. The umpires ignore the contact and do the right thing by keeping the ball in play. True or False?

6. Grady Sizemore of the Indians is on second base with one out. Victor Martinez rips a line drive base hit to White Sox center fielder Nick Swisher. Sizemore heads home and is called safe on a close play. Chicago catcher A. J. Pierzynski goes ballistic and is ejected from the game. Meanwhile, Martinez is advancing to second. Pierzynski fires to second and Martinez is called out. But since Pierzynski was ejected before the play, the umps correctly nullify the out and return Martinez to first base. True or False?

7. The Red Sox have Dustin Pedroia on third base when J. D. Drew hits a long fly ball that is caught by Orioles' right fielder Nick Markakis. Pedroia scores easily. After the first pitch to David Ortiz, the Orioles appeal that Pedroia left the base too soon. The umps properly allow Pedroia's run to score because no appeal can be upheld after a pitch has been made. True or False?

8. San Diego pitcher Jake Peavy is struck on the knee by a line drive. Padres skipper Bud Black comes out to check his pitcher. He decides Peavy is okay and returns to the dugout. Nationals' batter Ryan Zimmerman singles, and Black rushes back out to consult with Peavy. Because Black came out twice in the same inning to visit his pitcher, the umps properly remove Peavy from the game. True or False?

9. In the top of the seventh inning at Wrigley Field in Chicago, Daniel Murphy of the Mets hits a three-run homer which puts New York ahead, 5-3. With one out in the bottom of the seventh, a heavy downpour forces the umpires to call the game. The Cubs luck out because the score now reverts to the last completed inning, giving the Cubs a 3-2 win. True or False?

24

10. Prince Fielder of the Brewers hits a weak grounder along the first base line in foul territory. To prevent the ball from rolling into fair territory he throws his helmet at the ball and deflects it farther foul. The umps declare the ball dead and call Fielder out. They did the right thing. True or False?

QUIZ 6

Answers on page 73

1. Twenty-four players have 10,000 or more at-bats in the major leagues. Among these hitters, who posted the lowest career batting average with a .258 mark: Luis Aparicio, Rabbit Maranville, Cal Ripken, or Dave Winfield?

2. Eight left-handed pitchers have 2,500 or more career strikeouts. Collect ten points if you can identify four of these lefty hurlers.

3. Which one of these Rookie of the Year award recipients never won an MVP award: Dick Allen, Thurman Munson, Rod Carew, Billy Williams, or Orlando Cepeda?

4. Since 1900, only three pitchers have led their league in shutouts for three consecutive seasons, including Walter Johnson (1913–1915) of the Senators and Grover Alexander (1915–1917) of the Phillies. Who is the only other hurler to accomplish this feat: Sandy Koufax, Roger Clemens, Bob Gibson, or Fernando Valenzuela?

5. Since 1900, 13 different pitchers have had a 30-win season in the major leagues — 12 right-handers and one lefty. Collect ten points if you can identify five of these 30-game winners.

6. From 1900 through 2008, there have been six league batting champions whose last name begins with the letter "O." Collect ten points if you can name three of the six players. A clue: three of them won it in the American League and three in the National League.

7. Only five switch-hitters have led their league in runs batted in since 1900, with all five accomplishing the feat since 1956. Collect two points for each switch-batter you can identify who led either the American League or National League in runs batted in.

8. Barry Bonds is one of two players to have a 50-homer season and a 50-stolen base campaign during his major league career. Who is the only other player to match this feat: Willie Mays, Brady Anderson, Alex Rodriguez, Sammy Sosa, or Luis Gonzalez?

9. Against which pitcher did Joe Carter hit his walk-off home run to win the 1993 World Series for the Toronto Blue Jays: Stan Williams, Mitch Williams, Dave Williams, or Lefty Williams?

10. Nine players have clubbed 50 or more doubles in back-to-back seasons in the major leagues. Which one of the following players did not accomplish this feat: Todd Helton, Craig Biggio, Albert Pujols, or Garret Anderson?

CROSSWORD PUZZLE 3

Answer on page 75

ACROSS

1 He managed the Indians to the A.L. Central Division title in 2007

6 Mordecai "Three Finger" ____

9 Terry ____ was the catcher for the 1984 Padres

10 This team traded outfielder Jason Bay to the Boston Red Sox during the 2008 season

11 Famed baseball writer Lardner

12 Home runs with the bases loaded (2 wds.)

14 Nevada city that's home of the Triple-A "51s"

15 Where Ted Williams played his home games

18 Joe DiMaggio was "The ____ Clipper"

20 When a batter goes hitless for a dozen games, he's ____ (going bad)

23 Mickey Mantle was one, as was 18 Across

24 An outstanding third baseman, ____ Williams

26 Hall of Fame second baseman Eddie ____

27 Fans in this state took pride in their 2001 World Series champions

28 The Indians' Al ____ was A.L. MVP in 1953

29 Those who have not played a lot may show some ____ when they bat, field, or pitch

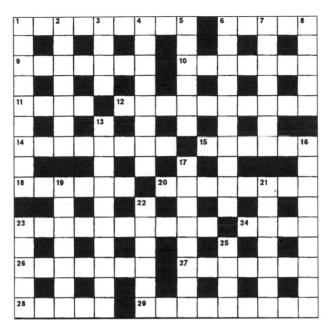

DOWN

1 Former Oakland Athletics' reliever Dennis ____

2 Frames in a baseball game

3 This____ in Baseball was once hosted by Mel Allen

4 Some Little Leaguers might ____ (fantasize) about becoming major league stars

5 Increase in size as big league baseball has done, growing from 16 to 30 teams

6 Plays exhibition games in small towns, like they did in the old days

7 To hang on is to barely ____ an opponent

8 Defeats narrowly, ____ out

13 This medium has enriched major league baseball enormously

16 The second games of doubleheaders

17 1992–1993 World Series winners

19 Graig ____ was an All-Star at third for the Yankees

21 A team that's far behind is said to be this (3 wds.)

22 A pitcher who attempts to finish a game for a starter or middle reliever

23 Onetime Yankee DH Gamble

25 Hall of Fame right fielder ____ Cuyler

QUIZ 7

Answers on page 75

True or False Trivia — Five points for each correct answer.

1. Mickey Mantle is the only switch-hitter with 500 or more career home runs?

2. Hank Aaron is the only major league player to hit more than 600 doubles and home runs during his career?

3. During the two seasons in which Ted Williams won the Triple Crown in the American League, he was not voted the A.L. MVP in either campaign?

4. Babe Ruth is the only major leaguer to record both a 20-win season as a pitcher and a 20-home run season as a batter during his career?

5. Red Sox pitcher Bob Stanley surrendered the home run to Yankee shortstop Bucky Dent in the 1978 playoff game to decide the A.L. East title?

6. Darin Erstad is the only player to win a Gold Glove award at different positions?

7. Reggie Jackson is the only player to hit three home runs in one World Series game?

8. In 3,948 innings pitched in the major leagues, Hall of Famer Jim Palmer never allowed a grand slam?

9. Randy Johnson was the first pitcher to win a Cy Young Award in both the American and National Leagues?

10. Tom Seaver's last major league victory came as a member of the Boston Red Sox?

11. Bobby Bonds and Barry Bonds are the only father and son duo to have a 30-homer season in the major leagues?

12. Former Red Sox slugger Tony Conigliaro is the youngest player to win a league home run title?

13. During the 1970s (1970–1979), no player hit more home runs than Willie Stargell's 296 for the Pittsburgh Pirates?

14. Sandy Koufax was the first pitcher to win three Cy Young Awards?

15. The Yankees and A's are the only two franchises to win three consecutive World Series titles?

16. Hall of Famer George Sisler is the all-time single-season hit leader with 257?

17. Rickey Henderson is the only player to steal 100 or more bases in a season three times during his big league career?

18. Dave Stewart was the last major league pitcher to be a 20-game winner four years in a row?

19. Bruce Sutter was the first relief pitcher to record 40 or more saves in a season?

20. Pete Rose holds the record for most career at-bats with more than 14,000?

Kinerisms from the Booth

Former New York Mets broadcaster Ralph Kiner, who made it to the Hall of Fame as a player, has often been spoofed for the "Kinerisms" that flowed from him during games. Here are ten gems by Kiner:

No. 10 — "The reason the Mets have played so well at Shea Stadium this season is that they have the best home record in baseball." **No. 9** — "And on this Father's Day, we again wish you all a happy birthday." **No. 8** — "We'll be right back with Mets baseball, right after the season is over." **No. 7** — "Todd Hundley walked intensely his last time up." **No. 6** — "They have been welding a very hot bat." **No. 5** — "There's Bonilla with his 23rd walk of the season. He's third in the National League in that department. The leader is Mark Grace with 23." **No. 4** — "David Cone is the pitcher of the year for the month of July." **No. 3** —After one umpire overruled another, Kiner said: "That never happens, unless it's a vagrant violation." **No. 2** — "We'll be back after this word from Manufacturer's Hangover." **No. 1** — "The ball is hit deep to right field. Way back. Way back. Going...going...it is gone...and is caught." **No. 1A** — "That's the great thing about baseball. You never know exactly what's going on."

RULES CHALLENGE 3

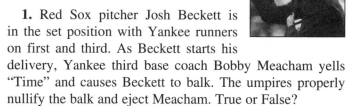

Answers on page 77

1. Red Sox pitcher Josh Beckett is in the set position with Yankee runners on first and third. As Beckett starts his delivery, Yankee third base coach Bobby Meacham yells "Time" and causes Beckett to balk. The umpires properly nullify the balk and eject Meacham. True or False?

2. The Astros have two outs with Lance Berkman on second when Hunter Pence hits an inside-the-park home run. Berkman misses the plate and Pence is called "safe" on a close play at the plate. Cubs' catcher Geovany Soto appeals and Berkman is called out. The umpires should allow Pence's run to score since the appeal was made after his run scored. True or False?

3. Michael Young is batting for the Rangers with two strikes. He swings at the next pitch and tips the ball. The ball goes directly onto the catcher's protector of Tigers' receiver Brandon Inge. It then bounces off Inge's chest before he catches it in his mitt. The umpire should call Young out. True or False?

4. Brad Hawpe of the Colorado Rockies taps a weak grounder along the first-base line in foul territory. The ball rolls up to and strikes his bat lying on the ground. The ball deflects into fair territory where it is gloved by Florida Marlins' pitcher Scott Olsen who throws to first baseman Mike Jacobs for the out. The umpires should rule Hawpe out on this play. True or False?

5. Carlos Pena of the Rays smashes a hot ground ball to Toronto first baseman Lyle Overbay who is able to get a glove on the ball and knock it down. Overbay has trouble picking up the ball but manages to grab it with his bare hand. He dives to tag the base, but he tags the base with an empty glove as he holds the ball in his bare hand. Regardless, Pena should be called out. True or False?

6. The Kansas City Royals' David DeJesus is on first and attempts to steal second base. Orioles' catcher Ramon

Hernandez cocks his arm to throw to second and accidentally strikes plate umpire Joe West in the mask. Hernandez hesitates briefly then fires to second too late to retire DeJesus. However, DeJesus should be called out because of the umpire's interference. True or False?

7. A ball boy is stationed against the fence down the left field line at Fenway Park in Boston. Toronto Blue Jays manager John Gibbons refuses to put his team on the field arguing that the ball boy and his chair pose a physical hazard to his fielders. After a reasonable amount of time, the umpire-in-chief properly forfeits the game to the Red Sox. True or False?

8. Chipper Jones, on first base for the Braves, is off and running on the pitch. As he races for second, his helmet falls to the ground. Jeff Francoeur, the batter, hits the pitch toward the hole between first and second, and the ball strikes Jones' helmet. Reds' second baseman Brandon Phillips is unable to field the ball for the routine putout. The umpires correctly rule Francoeur out on the play. True or False?

9. Alfonso Soriano is on third base for the Cubs with one out. Derrek Lee is batting with two strikes when Soriano, stealing home, is struck by the pitch in the strike zone. Soriano should be called out and Lee should remain at bat. True or False?

10. Alfonso Soriano is on third base with two outs. Derrek Lee is batting with an 0-2 count when Soriano, stealing home, is struck by the pitch. The umpires correctly call Lee out for strike three and Soriano's run does not count. True or False?

DID YOU KNOW . . . that on August 4, 1982, Joel Youngblood became the only major league player to collect a hit with two different teams on the same day? He singled for the Mets against the Cubs in a day game before being traded to Montreal and registering a pinch-hit for the Expos against the Phillies in a night game.

PHOTO QUIZ 2

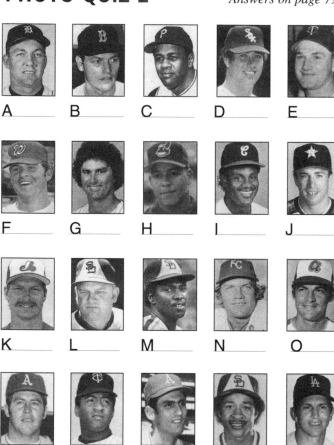

Answers on page 79

A_____ B_____ C_____ D_____ E_____

F_____ G_____ H_____ I_____ J_____

K_____ L_____ M_____ N_____ O_____

P_____ Q_____ R_____ S_____ T_____

1 Jeff Bagwell	**9** Jim Hunter	**17** Denny McLain
2 Craig Biggio	**10** Randy Johnson	**18** Manny Ramirez
3 George Brett	**11** Jim Kaat	**19** Ozzie Smith
4 Steve Carlton	**12** Al Kaline	**20** Sammy Sosa
5 Rollie Fingers	**13** H. Killebrew	**21** Willie Stargell
6 Carlton Fisk	**14** Tony LaRussa	**22** Don Sutton
7 Rich Gossage	**15** Victor Martinez	**23** Luis Tiant
8 Tony Gwynn	**16** Eddie Mathews	**24** Don Zimmer

QUIZ 8

Answers on page 79

Who Am I?

1. I finished among the top five MVP vote-getters in the American League from 1950 through 1956, winning the award three times. I was the first player to club a pinch-hit World Series home run. I hit 358 career home runs and fanned only 414 times during my career. I was elected to the Hall of Fame in 1972. My first name is Lawrence. Who am I?

2. I played 22 years in the majors, beginning with the Houston Astros and retiring with the Oakland A's. I won five Gold Glove awards and two National League MVP honors. I hit 268 home runs and stole 689 bases. I played on four pennant winners and two World Series champions, collecting the game-winning hit in a memorable Game 7 Fall Classic. Who am I?

3. I won seven batting titles and hit 475 lifetime home runs. I hit only .256 in 86 World Series at-bats, yet I was a member of three World Series–winning clubs. In one of my most productive seasons, I fell one home run short of capturing the Triple Crown. I started All-Star games at four different positions (left field, center field, right field, first base). I finished second in MVP voting four times and captured the honor three times. I was elected to the Hall of Fame in 1969. Who am I?

4. During my first full season in the majors, I was elected my league's Rookie of the Year and Most Valuable Player. I set an A.L. rookie record with 47 doubles. I started my career with the Boston Red Sox and ended it with the San Diego Padres. I am the only player to hit a grand slam in an All-Star game. Who am I?

5. I have 194 career victories as a big league pitcher to my credit, including a perfect game and a 19-strikeout performance. I am the only pitcher to win 20 or more games in a season for both the New York Yankees and the New York Mets. Who am I?

6. I am the only third baseman in baseball history to have multiple seasons in which I hit .300 with 30-plus homers while winning a Gold Glove. I clubbed 342 home runs during my career. During a nine-year stretch in my prime, I averaged 28 homers and 103 RBIs per season as one of the game's most productive third basemen. During a memorable season, I was known for jumping and clicking my heels after each of my club's victories. My uniform No. 10 was retired by the club I played the longest for. Who am I?

7. I won two league MVP awards, yet I am not in the Hall of Fame. I began my major league career as a catcher but later moved to center field where I captured five Gold Glove awards. I finished second in my league in home runs three times while winning two HR titles and ending my career with 398. I played in 740 consecutive games from 1981 to 1986. Who am I?

8. I saved 30 or more games in a season 10 times in the major leagues. I saved 20 or more games in a season with five different clubs. I totaled 478 saves from the start of my career with the Chicago Cubs to the end of my time in the majors with the Montreal Expos. I surrendered a walk-off home run to Steve Garvey in Game 4 of the 1984 National League Championship Series. Who am I?

9. Since 1931 when the Baseball Writers Association of America began MVP voting, I was the first National League catcher to win the honor. I hit 236 lifetime homers including a career high 37 in 1930. I closed out my 20 years in the big leagues with the New York Giants. I was inducted into the Hall of Fame in 1955. I hit a famous home run to help my club win the pennant, most commonly referred to as the "Homer in the Gloamin.'" Who am I?

10. My first major league hit was a grand slam. I slugged a home run for eight different teams, including 20 or more in a season for five teams. I hit 332 career homers and stole 461 bases. I hit 30 home runs and stole 30 bases in the same season five times and became the first player to accomplish the feat in both leagues. Who am I?

QUIZ 9

Answers on page 80

1. There are 14 players with 600 or more career doubles. Among these players, who is the only one not to lead his league in two-base hits during his career: George Brett, Carl Yastrzemski, Pete Rose, or Barry Bonds?

2. Collect ten points if you can identify the two pitchers who have won three or more consecutive Cy Young Awards. Collect five points for each correct answer.

3. Excluding the designated hitter, a player has won consecutive MVP awards at every position in baseball. Collect ten points if you can identify a player who won back-to-back MVP honors at four of the nine defensive positions.

Rickey Henderson

4. There have been four former players elected to the Hall of Fame whose last name begins with the letter "Y." Collect ten points if you can identify three of these four players.

5. During his 25 years in the major leagues, Rickey Henderson amassed more than 3,000 hits, 1,400 stolen bases, 2,000 walks, and 2,000 runs scored. He reached these totals while playing with nine different teams. Name six of the teams Henderson played for during his career to collect ten points.

6. Which manager has been ejected from a game the most times in his career: Billy Martin, Earl Weaver, Lou Piniella, or Bobby Cox?

7. Four players have struck out 2,000 or more times in the majors. Collect ten points if you can identify three of these four batters.

8. Pitcher Jim Kaat is one of 11 major league players to win ten or more consecutive Gold Glove awards. Collect one point for each of the ten other players to accomplish this feat you can identify.

9. Since 1900, there have been three players with a last name of "Williams" who have won a league batting title. Collect ten points if you can identify two of these three players named Williams.

10. Who is the only player to slam a home run for his 3,000th career hit: Pete Rose, Stan Musial, Wade Boggs, or Hank Aaron?

RULES CHALLENGE 4

Answers on page 82

1. The Royals have Jose Guillen on third and one out when Alex Gordon hits a long fly ball foul down the third-base line near the wall 300 feet from home plate. Marcus Thames, the Tigers' left fielder, is under the ball preparing to make the catch when the ball is touched by a fan reaching out of the stands. The ball falls uncaught while Guillen tags up and scores. The umpires rule Gordon out because of spectator interference but properly allow Guillen to score because of the distance from home to where the interference occurred. True or False?

2. The A's have Jack Cust on third with two outs and no count on Eric Chavez. The Oakland third baseman takes ball one as Cust attempts to steal home on the pitch. As the Rays' catcher Dioner Navarro is about to tag Cust, who is sliding into the plate, Chavez interferes with Navarro's attempt to tag the runner. The umpire rules interference on the play and correctly calls Chavez out because there were two outs at the time of the interference. True or False?

3. In the late innings of a close game between the Angels and Mariners, the Angels have Gary Matthews, Jr., on third base. To guard against a passed ball or wild pitch,

Mariners' manager Jim Riggleman brings in outfielder Wladimir Balentien to play behind catcher Kenji Johjima and the umpire. Angels' manager Mike Scioscia argues that this is illegal, but the umps do the right thing by allowing Balentien to play behind Johjima in foul territory. True or False?

4. The Yankees' Robinson Cano is batting with a 3-1 count when manager Joe Girardi emerges from the dugout and points out to the ump that Bobby Abreu should be the batter. Girardi summons Abreu to replace Cano and inherit the 3-1 count. The umpire makes the right decision by allowing the exchange. True or False?

5. The Mets' Carlos Delgado makes the third out of the inning. He injures himself as he swings and misses strike three. As the trainer is checking him out in the dugout, a reserve player assumes Delgado's position at first base to warm up the infielders. Delgado is deemed okay to continue and goes back to first base before the start of the inning. Cubs' manager Lou Piniella argues that the reserve player must be the new first baseman since he assumed that position. Piniella has a good argument. True or False?

6. Khalil Greene of the Padres hits a double, scoring Adrian Gonzalez. Phillies' catcher Carlos Ruiz picks up the bat and appeals to the umpire that the pine tar on the bat exceeds the 18-inch limitation. The umpire agrees and properly calls Greene out and returns Gonzalez to his base. True or False?

7. Boston manager Terry Francona and Texas skipper Ron Washington meet with the umpires at home plate to discuss the ground rules and exchange lineup cards. After the discussion has ended and both managers have left the home plate area, the plate umpire discovers that the visiting manager (Francona) has listed Mike Lowell twice in the lineup card. The umpire should not say anything, but when Lowell comes to bat he should call him out for batting out of turn. True or False?

8. In the top of the seventh inning, the Blue Jays are batting when Vernon Wells walks and Scott Rolen doubles to right. At that point the umpire realizes that the Indians are playing without right fielder Franklin Gutierrez, who remained in the clubhouse for medical treatment. Because no action may take place with less than nine defensive players on the field, the umpire should negate the efforts of Wells and Rolen and start the inning over. True or False?

9. After a run-saving catch by Dodgers outfielder Andruw Jones, Rockies manager Clint Hurdle approaches the umpire to complain that he thinks Jones is using an illegal glove — one that measures more than 12 inches from top to bottom. Upon close examination, the umpire agrees and correctly nullifies the out and returns Matt Holliday, the Rockies' runner, to his base. True or False?

10. The Twins have Joe Mauer on first and Michael Cuddyer, an improper batter, at the plate. Mauer advances to second on a wild pitch. Cuddyer then laces a line drive to right field to score Mauer. White Sox manager Ozzie Guillen properly appeals the batting out of order, and the umpire upholds the appeal for the first out. The umpire then puts Mauer back on second since his advance on the wild pitch was legal. The entire situation was properly handled. True or False?

You Make the Call

Situation: A pitcher must pitch to at least one batter before being relieved. A relief pitcher, coming in with two out, picks a runner off base before he actually pitches to a batter. Must he face the first hitter the next inning?

Answer: No. While the rule stipulates that a pitcher must pitch to one complete batter, it adds "or until the offensive side is retired."

Situation: A batter pops a foul fly into the first row of the third-base stands. The shortstop, racing over to make the play, reaches in to make the catch, but the ball brushes a fan's hands. Still, the shortstop makes the catch. Is the batter out?

Answer: No. The ball is dead when contact is made by a fan in the stands. If the ball had struck a fan's hand outside the stands, the batter would be out — interference.

Players Who Have Hit Two
Grand Slams in One Game

Player, Team	Date	AB	H	RBI
Tony Lazzeri, Yankees	May 24, 1936	5	4	11

HR hit off George Turbeville (2nd inn.) and Malton Bullock (5th inn.) of the Philadelphia A's

Jim Tabor, Red Sox	July 4, 1939	4	3	9

HR hit off George Caster (3rd inn.) and Chubby Dean (6th inn.) of the Philadelphia A's

Rudy York, Red Sox	July 27, 1946	5	3	10

HR hit off Bob Muncrief (2nd inn.) and Tex Shirley (5th inn.) of the St. Louis Browns

Jim Gentile, Orioles	May 9, 1961	3	2	9

HR hit off Pedro Ramos (1st inn.) and Paul Giel (2nd inn.) of the Minnesota Twins

Tony Cloninger, Braves	July 3, 1966	5	3	9

HR hit off Bob Priddy (1st inn.) and Ray Sadecki (4th inn.) of the San Francisco Giants

Jim Northrup, Tigers	June 24, 1968	4	2	8

HR hit off Eddie Fisher (5th inn.) and Billy Rohr (6th inn.) of the Cleveland Indians

Frank Robinson, Orioles	June 26, 1970	4	2	8

HR hit off Joe Coleman (5th inn.) and Joe Grzenda (6th inn.) of the Washington Senators

Robin Ventura, White Sox	Sept. 4, 1995	5	3	8

HR hit off Dennis Cook (4th inn.) and Danny Darwin (5th inn.) of the Texas Rangers

Chris Hoiles, Orioles	Aug. 14, 1998	5	3	8

HR hit off Charles Nagy (3rd inn.) and Ron Villone (8th inn.) of the Cleveland Indians

Fernando Tatis, Cardinals	April 23, 1999	5	2	8

HRs hit off Chan Ho Park (both in 3rd inn.) of the Los Angeles Dodgers

Nomar Garciaparra, Bsn.	May 10, 1999	4	3	10

HR hit off Brett Hinchliffe (1st inn.) and Eric Weaver (8th inn.) of the Seattle Mariners

Bill Mueller, Red Sox	July 29, 2003	5	3	9

HR hit off Aaron Fultz (7th inn.) and Jay Powell (8th inn.) of the Texas Rangers

CROSSWORD PUZZLE 4

Answer on page 84

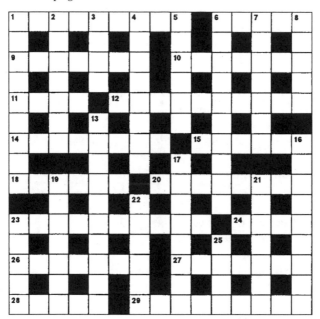

ACROSS

1 Dodger right-hander who was N.L. starter in 2006 All-Star game

6 Ex-catcher Bob _____ is the father of Bret and Aaron and son of Ray, all major leaguers

9 The A in BA or ERA

10 A pitcher who isn't bringing it is said to have "_____ on the ball"

11 Former first baseman _____ Karros, who won N.L. Rookie of the Year in 1992

12 Slang for a vicious, low line drive (2 wds.)

14 For major leaguers, _____ camp takes place in spring

15 A player who likes to show off is called this

18 Middle name of Hall of Fame second baseman Nellie Fox

20 Description of a first-class player

23 Mets outfielder in 2007 who hit .291 with 10 home runs

24 Another outfielder, Joe _____, had his best years with the A's

26 Bud Selig once owned this club

27 Walking a batter, ____ a pass

28 Tony Kubek and Bill Skowron were once ____

29 One who is quick on the base paths

DOWN

1 Where the Pittsburgh Pirates have trained for many years

2 God Bless ____ is a popular tune at ball parks

3 An old refrain: "Spahn and Sain, and ____ for rain"

4 Heckling another ball player

5 Roger Maris hit 61 home runs in 1961 as a ____

6 Sends at least nine batters to the plate in an inning (2 wds.)

7 Left out of the lineup

8 Martinez who spent years as a DH with the Seattle Mariners

13 Vin Scully and Hawk Harrelson are two

16 Charlie ____ played second base alongside first baseman Hank Greenberg on the old Tigers

17 The New York Mets took a ____ (sudden, sharp drop) at the end of the 2007 season

19 Strand, ____ ____ base (2 wds.)

21 Ancient Wrigley Field remains a ____ attraction in Chicago

22 If you break them while a pitch nears the plate and you miss the ball, it's generally ruled a strike

23 Old-time Boston Braves infielder ____ Sisti, who was involved in a controversial play against the Indians in the 1948 World Series

25 Ichiro Suzuki has ____ the whole field, hitting the ball in every direction

---

They Said It . . .

Lefty O'Doul, former two-time N.L. batting champ, talking about player salaries, especially the $90,000 that Willie Mays was supposed to be getting in 1962: *"When I hit .397 in the majors, they gave me a $500 raise. Then in 1932, I slumped — slumped, mind you — to .367 and they cut me by $1,000."*

Ted Williams, the majors' last .400 hitter: *"I knew it was time to quit when I was on second base and third base looked a mile away. I would hope the next batter would hit a homer so I could trot around."*

QUIZ 10

Answers on page 85

Uniform Numbers

1. Uniform No. 8 was retired by the New York Yankees in honor of two Hall of Famers. Collect five points for each of these players you can identify who wore No. 8 for the Yankees.

2. There have been seven major league Hall of Fame players who wore uniform No. 5. Collect ten points if you can identify three of these players.

3. There are two Hall of Fame left-handed pitchers who won three or more Cy Young Awards, and both wore uniform No. 32. Collect five points for each of these pitchers you can identify.

Eddie Gaedel

4. Which of the following Hall of Famers did not wear uniform No. 8: Willie Stargell, Carl Yastrzemski, Joe Morgan, or Al Kaline?

5. True or False. Hall of Fame players Frank Robinson, Don Sutton, Lou Brock, and Mike Schmidt all wore uniform No. 20?

6. Besides Jackie Robinson, whose No. 42 was retired by major league baseball, who is the only player to have his uniform number retired by three different clubs: Rollie Fingers, Reggie Jackson, Nolan Ryan, or Andre Dawson?

7. The two players to hit 70 or more home runs in a season (Barry Bonds 73 in 2001 and Mark McGwire 70 in 1998) both wore the same uniform number. What number was it: 21, 24, 25, or 27?

8. Match the following players with the uniform numbers they wore during their playing career in the majors. Collect two points for each correct match.

Ernie Banks	45
Dave Winfield	22
Jim Palmer	14
Bob Gibson	19
Bob Feller	31

9. Which major league player wore his birthdate (name and number) on the back of his jersey: Don August, Carlos May, Milt May, or Lee May?

10. When Bill Veeck used midget Eddie Gaedel as a pinch hitter on August 19, 1951, with the St. Louis Browns, what number did Gaedel wear on the back of his uniform: 0, 1, 1/2, 1/4, or 1/8?

Name That Pitcher

Answers on page 84

A. I surrendered Bill Mazeroski's walk-off, World Series–winning home run in 1960. In 1962, I won Game 7 of the World Series against the Giants, getting Willie McCovey to hit a line drive out to second base with runners on second and third. Who am I?

B. I won three games in the 1968 World Series against the Cardinals, including Game 7 vs. Bob Gibson. Who am I?

C. I won 286 major league games and entered the Hall of Fame in 1976. I am the only pitcher in major league history to give up more than 500 career home runs. Who am I?

D. I had four 20-win seasons in the majors and won 184 career games, 181 of them with the Baltimore Orioles. I am the only pitcher to hit a grand slam in the World Series. Who am I?

E. I am one of only two pitchers to have two seasons with ten or more shutouts. I am one of two pitchers to win 30 or more games in a season three years in a row. I won 373 career games with three N.L. teams. Who am I?

CROSSWORD PUZZLE 5

Answer on page 85

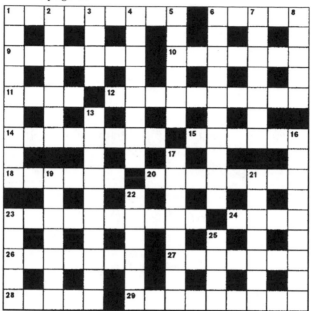

ACROSS

1 Pitch known as "Uncle Charlie"

6 A good pal on your team

9 Hall of Fame manager Tom _____ won two World Series titles

10 A walk-off grand slam will often _____ (save) a game for a team that was behind going into the last inning

11 Front-office guy

12 "Oil Can" who pitched for the Red Sox some years ago

14 Get more runs than an opponent

15 "Duke" played center field and hit a lot of home runs for the Dodgers

18 He has been a strong force on offense for the Indians, _____ Hafner

20 Most inexperienced, like the rawest rookie on the team

23 He managed the Dodgers in Brooklyn and Los Angeles

24 They won their first National League pennant in 1969

26 Taller and thinner

27 Makes contact, ___ _____ (2 wds.) wood on the ball

28 Took a cut and missed, as the late Dizzy Dean would say when he broadcast games

29 Bleacher fans should wear this for protection on hot, midsummer days

DOWN

1 A batter who is retired when not swinging at a third strike is ____ ____ (2 wds.) looking

2 A manager who has lost the ____ of his players is in big trouble

3 Legendary skipper ____ Weaver

4 Non-professionals, like baseball's earliest players

5 The ____ pitcher gets an "L"

6 He won 20 games for the Dodgers in 1969 and tossed a no-hitter in 1970

7 The playing field for baseball is called a ____

8 A manager hates to see his pitcher ____ (give up) a walk at a critical point in the game

13 Returning a player to the roster from the disabled list

16 Gambler Arnold ____ was said to be behind the 1919 Black Sox scandal

17 Location of long-gone Ebbets Field

19 Where Hank Aaron belted many of his big league home runs

21 To ____ ____ count is to knot it at 1-and-1 or 2-and-2

22 Roy Oswalt's 2008 club

23 Both David ____ and David Cone tossed perfect games for the Yankees

25 A pitcher and his catcher need to be in ____ to get the best results

Bob Uecker's Career Highlights

Former catcher and current Brewers announcer Bob Uecker is a fast man with a quip. For example: "I remember my frustrating days as a catcher in Philadelphia. The general manager told me they had a very young pitching staff and asked me to help the best way I could. He asked me to quit. Gene Mauch was one of my favorite managers. He used to say, "Get a bat and stop this rally." Asked when he knew his playing career with the Atlanta Braves was over, Uecker smiled and responded, "When manager Luman Harris told me no visitors were allowed in the clubhouse. The highlights of my career? I had two — the day I got an intentional walk from Sandy Koufax, and when I got out of a rundown against the Mets."

RULES CHALLENGE 5

Answers on page 86

1. A pitch grazes the sleeve of the Diamondbacks' Stephen Drew. Because the pitch did not actually hit him, the umpire should call the pitch a "ball" and refuse to award Drew first base. True or False?

2. The Brewers have Ryan Braun on first base and no outs with J. J. Hardy in the batter's box. Braun takes off with the pitch and has second base stolen easily. Hardy swings and misses the pitch that hits him. The umpire should call a strike on Hardy but allow Braun to stay at second base since he would have stolen the base anyway. True or False?

3. The Angels have Garret Anderson on third and Brandon Wood on second with one out when Vladimir Guerrero hits a double to drive in both runners. Anderson, the runner on third, fails to touch home plate. Wood, running behind him, touches the plate. Realizing he missed the plate, Anderson returns to touch it before Twins' catcher Joe Mauer appeals. The umpire should allow Anderson's run to count since he touched the plate before Mauer made the appeal. True or False?

4. Jim Thome of the White Sox hits a foul ball deep into the right-field stands. The umpire calls Thome out because his back foot was completely out of the batter's box when he made contact with the ball. Thome argues that because the ball was foul, he should not be called out. The umpire made the proper decision by calling him out. True or False?

5. With two outs, Reds' batter Joey Votto hits a grand slam. While rounding the bases, Votto misses second base. The umpire upholds the appeal and rules Votto out for the third out. The three runners on base, however, all touch the plate. The plate umpire should allow all three runs to score. True or False?

6. The Cardinals have runners on first and second with one out when Rick Ankiel hits a shot down the right-field line. Albert Pujols, the runner on second, scores, but Troy

Glaus, the runner on first, is thrown out at the plate. Ankiel advances to second on the play but is declared out on appeal for missing first base. No runs should score on this play. True or False?

7. Travis Hafner of the Indians is batting with the bases loaded and no outs when he hits a pop fly between home and third base. The plate umpire yells, "Infield Fly if fair." The ball falls to the ground untouched on foul territory then bounces into fair territory and settles in fair ground in front of the third-base bag. Hafner should not be called out on the play because the ball landed in foul territory before rolling fair. True or False?

8. Cubs' pitcher Carlos Zambrano has a problem releasing the ball and fires it into the ground a few inches in front of home plate. The ball bounces into the strike zone where Adam Dunn swings and clubs a home run. The umpire correctly disallows the home run and calls the pitch a "ball" claiming a batter cannot hit a pitch that bounces in the dirt. True or False?

9. Miguel Tejada of the Astros squares around to bunt. His right foot is touching the batter's box line and home plate. He lays down a bunt and is called "safe" at first. But Tejada should be called out since part of his foot was touching home plate. True or False?

10. Ryan Howard of the Phillies gloves a fly ball in foul territory on the spectator side of the first-base line. However, a fan reaches into Howard's glove and takes the ball for a souvenir. The fan does this before Howard attempts to transfer the ball from his glove. Regardless, since Howard had control and secure possession of the ball, this should be ruled a catch. True or False?

Factoid: On May 1, 1991, Rickey Henderson stole his 939th career base in the major leagues to break Lou Brock's all-time mark. Henderson finished with a lifetime total of 1,406, including 867 as a member of the A's, 326 with the Yankees, 91 with the Padres, 42 with the Mets, 31 with Seattle, 22 with Toronto, 16 with the Angels, 8 with Boston, and 3 with the Dodgers.

QUIZ 11

Answers on page 89

1. The San Francisco Giants have had six different National League home run champions in their club's history, including Barry Bonds, who paced the N.L. in homers twice as a member of the Giants. Collect two points for each of the other five you can name.

2. Since 1900, who is the only player to collect 200 or more singles in one season: Pete Rose, Ichiro Suzuki, Rod Carew, or Lloyd Waner?

3. Who is the only pitcher with 300 or more career victories to post only one 20-win season during his career: Nolan Ryan, Greg Maddux, Gaylord Perry, or Don Sutton?

4. The fewest grand slams hit by a player with 500 or more career home runs are seven, a mark held by three sluggers. Hall of Famers Mel Ott and Willie Mays are two of these players. Who is the third member of the 500 Home Run Club to blast only seven lifetime bases-loaded homers: Mike Schmidt, Ted Williams, Hank Aaron, or Ken Griffey, Jr.?

5. Who holds the major league record for hitting the most home runs (14) against one team in a single season: Babe Ruth, Barry Bonds, Lou Gehrig, or Sammy Sosa?

6. Since 1990, who is the only player to drive in 300 combined runs in back-to-back seasons: Alex Rodriguez, Sammy Sosa, Manny Ramirez, or Juan Gonzalez?

7. In 1979, two players tied for the National League Most Valuable Player award. Collect five points for each of these MVP winners you can identify.

8. During his major league career, Frank Robinson hit 586 lifetime home runs with five different teams. Collect ten points if you can identify the three teams for which Robinson clubbed 30 or more homers in a season.

9. Since 1900, 25 players have reached the 3,000-hit plateau in their careers. Among those 25, only seven led their league in stolen bases. Collect ten points if you can identify three of the seven players who won a stolen-base title and collected 3,000 hits during their big league careers.

10. Since 1900, four pitchers have thrown a no-hitter with different teams, including Nolan Ryan, who tossed hitless games for the California Angels, Houston Astros, and Texas Rangers during his career. Collect ten points if you can identify one of the three other hurlers to accomplish this feat.

Players Who Teamed for Most Career Home Runs

Years	Players (HR)	Total
1954–1966	Hank Aaron (442) / Eddie Mathews (421)	863
1923–1934*	Babe Ruth (498) / Lou Gehrig (348)	846
1959–1972+	Willie Mays (413) / Willie McCovey (371)	784
1947–1961	Duke Snider (384) / Gil Hodges (361)	745
1974–1989	Jim Rice (382) / Dwight Evans (355)	737
1991–2005	Jeff Bagwell (469) / Craig Biggio (243)	712
1996–2007#	Andruw Jones (368) / Chipper Jones (338)	706
1960–1973†	Billy Williams (376) / Ron Santo (328)	704
1951–1963	Mickey Mantle (419) / Yogi Berra (283)	702

* From June 15, 1923, when Gehrig made his debut through end of 1934 season
+ From July 30, 1959, when McCovey made his debut through May 11, 1972, when Giants traded Mays to Mets
# From August 15, 1996, when Andruw Jones made his big league debut through end of 2007 season
† From September 20, 1960, when Williams was recalled by Cubs through end of 1973 season

Eddie Mathews, left, and Hank Aaron combined to club 863 home runs as teammates with the Milwaukee/Atlanta Braves

PHOTO QUIZ 3

Answers on page 90

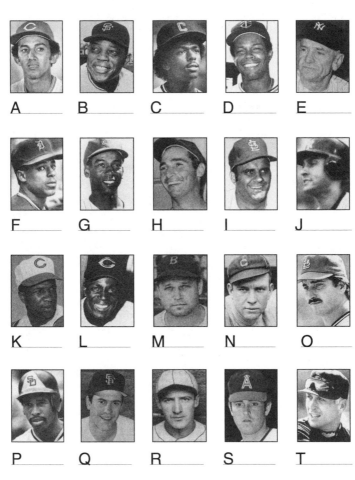

A ___ B ___ C ___ D ___ E ___

F ___ G ___ H ___ I ___ J ___

K ___ L ___ M ___ N ___ O ___

P ___ Q ___ R ___ S ___ T ___

1 Ernie Banks	**9** Keith Hernandez	**17** Frank Robinson
2 Bob Brenly	**10** Derek Jeter	**18** Alex Rodriguez
3 Rod Carew	**11** Sandy Koufax	**19** Nolan Ryan
4 Will Clark	**12** Willie Mays	**20** Tris Speaker
5 Dave Concepcion	**13** Joe McCarthy	**21** Casey Stengel
6 Cecil Fielder	**14** Joe Medwick	**22** Joe Torre
7 Jimmie Foxx	**15** Minnie Minoso	**23** Lou Whitaker
8 Julio Franco	**16** Cal Ripken	**24** Dave Winfield

QUIZ 12

Answers on page 90

1. In 2007, two major leaguers accomplished the rare feat of hitting 20 or more doubles, triples, and home runs while stealing 20 or more bases in the same season. Collect five points for each of these players you can identify.

2. Which player has the most seasons with 40 or more home runs: Barry Bonds, Babe Ruth, Hank Aaron, or Alex Rodriguez?

3. Ten players with 3,000 or more career hits did not win a league batting title. Collect one point for each of these ten batters you can identify.

4. Who was the last major league pitcher to work 300 or more innings in one season: Orel Hershiser, Randy Johnson, Steve Carlton, or Phil Niekro?

5. Which pitcher holds the record for most consecutive 200-strikeout seasons with nine: Roger Clemens, Nolan Ryan, Bert Blyleven, or Tom Seaver?

6. Since 1900, 22 different players have won back-to-back league batting titles. Who did not win consecutive hitting titles during his career: George Brett, Carl Yastrzemski, Nomar Garciaparra, or Dave Parker?

7. Only two players since 1900 have hit .400 or higher and not won a league batting title in the majors. Collect ten points if you can identify one of these hitters.

8. In 1985, a left-handed pitcher in the National League posted a 21-8 won-lost record with ten shutouts and an ERA of 1.93 but did not capture the N.L. Cy Young Award. Who was this pitcher: Steve Trout, John Tudor, Tom Browning, or Jerry Reuss?

9. During his career, Hank Aaron hit a home run off 13 different future Hall of Fame pitchers. Collect ten points if you can identify seven of these hurlers.

10. Which batter posted the most seasons with 150 or more RBI with seven: Babe Ruth, Jimmie Foxx, Lou Gehrig, or Hank Greenberg?

CROSSWORD PUZZLE 6

Answer on page 91

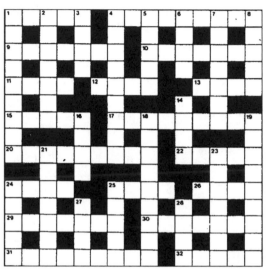

ACROSS

1 He has caught for the Mariners, _____ Johjima

4 Christy _____ won an amazing 37 games in 1908

9 A _____ is when management shuts the door on players

10 A shortstop, Bill _____ once managed the Dodgers

11 Cardinal great _____ Slaughter who's in the Hall of Fame

12 The regular major league season reaches the halfway mark during this month

13 The Giants play in San _____, as it is known in short

15 Pitch that climbs

17 Hall of Fame right-hander Grover _____

20 This Giant first baseman, dubbed "The Thrill," led the National League with 109 RBIs in 1988

22 Ken _____ was manager in Oakland 2003–2006

24 Be ahead

25 James _____ Jones was among the cast of *Field of Dreams*

26 "The Georgia Peach"

29 A pitcher who gets bombed by opposing batters is said to have been _____

30 He led the Cardinals to their World Series triumph in 2006

31 Left-hander who led the 1978 Yankees with a 25-3 record

32 "Cap" was player-manager for some great Cub teams in the long ago

DOWN

1 "Killer" went deep 573 times

2 Cubs right fielder Bill _____ on hit 29 and 33 homers in 1943 and 1944 to lead the National League

3 Cal Ripken earned the title of baseball's "_____ Man"

4 "Dice-K" is the nickname of Red Sox pitcher Daisuke _____

5 First baseman Bill _____ of the New York Giants hit .401 in 1930

6 The Tampa Bay Rays play in the A.L. _____ Division

7 Guided

8 Former flamethrower Ryan

14 Minor league teams serve as _____ clubs

16 _____ Sutcliffe won the 1984 N.L. Cy Young Award while with the Cubs

18 Righty reliever who was the A.L. Cy Young Award winner in 1992

19 Milwaukee Brewer who was the N.L. Rookie of the Year in 2007

21 A losing team will often _____ _ base (2 wds.) too many runners

23 Scores a run, _____ the plate

24 No major leaguer likes to be tabbed a _____

25 Bill Mazeroski's ninth-inning home run _____ (concluded) the 1960 World Series between the Pirates and Yankees

27 Felipe _____ was a manager in Montreal

28 Second baseman Jorge__ __ was an A.L. All-Star with the White Sox and Indians

DID YOU KNOW ... that former pitcher Mike Morgan holds the distinction of winning a game for the most different major league teams, 11? During his career, he won games with the A's (2), Yankees (7), Mariners (24), Orioles (1), Dodgers (33), Cubs (30), Cardinals (9), Reds (11), Twins (4), Rangers (13), and Diamondbacks (7). He also holds the mark for losing a game with 12 different clubs. He lost with the A's (13), Yankees (11), Blue Jays (3), Mariners (35), Orioles (6), Dodgers (36), Cubs (35), Cardinals (14), Reds (15), Twins (2), Rangers (10), and Diamondbacks (6). Combined record: 141-186.

QUIZ 13

Answers on page 92

Family Ties

1. Who are the only brothers to win a Cy Young Award: Pedro and Ramon Martinez, Joe and Phil Niekro, Jim and Gaylord Perry, or Mike and Greg Maddux?

2. Name the only brothers in major league history to win league batting titles: Harry and Dixie Walker, Matty and Felipe Alou, or Paul and Lloyd Waner?

3. Besides the Boyers, Ken and Clete, who won Gold Glove awards as third basemen, who are the only other brothers to capture Gold Glove honors as the best defensive player at his position: Cal and Billy Ripken, Roberto and Sandy Alomar, Jr., Rick and Paul Reuschel, or Tony and Chris Gwynn?

4. Who are the only brothers elected to the Hall of Fame: Rick and Wes Ferrell, George and Ken Brett, Lloyd and Paul Waner, or Joe and Dom DiMaggio?

5. Identify the only father and son major league players to steal 50 or more bases in a single season: George and Dick Sisler, Maury and Bump Wills, Barry and Bobby Bonds, or Tim Raines, Sr., and Tim Raines, Jr.?

6. On September 22, 1963, brothers Matty, Felipe, and Jesus Alou all played in the outfield at the same time for the same team in a game. For which team did they accomplish this feat: St. Louis Cardinals, Milwaukee Braves, Houston Colt .45s, or San Francisco Giants?

7. Who are the only brothers to hurl official complete-game no-hitters in the major leagues: Bob and Ken Forsch, Dizzy and Paul Dean, Al and Mark Leiter, or Jim and Dennis O'Toole?

8. Which brother duo combined for the most career victories with 539: Phil and Joe Niekro, or Gaylord and Jim Perry?

9. Sandy Alomar, Jr., and Roberto Alomar are the only brothers to win All-Star game MVP awards. Who are the only father and son All-Star game MVP recipients: Bobby and Barry Bonds, Ken Griffey, Sr., and Ken Griffey, Jr., Cecil and Prince Fielder, or Gus and Buddy Bell?

10. Who are the only brothers to hit a home run in the same World Series game: Tommie and Hank Aaron, Felipe and Matty Alou, Ken and Clete Boyer, or Ken and George Brett?

RULES CHALLENGE 6

Answers on page 93

1. The Red Sox have Jacoby Ellsbury on first base and no outs when Jason Varitek hits a fly ball to Indians' center fielder Grady Sizemore. As the ball hits Sizemore's glove, Ellsbury tags and breaks for second. Sizemore juggles the ball but makes the catch before the ball hits the ground. The Indians appeal that Ellsbury left the base before the ball was caught. The umpires correctly call Ellsbury out for leaving the base too soon. True or False?

2. In the bottom of the ninth inning, the White Sox and Tigers are tied 5-5 at U.S. Cellular Field. Chicago has two outs with the bases loaded when Jermaine Dye homers over the center-field wall. The runners from third and second cross the plate. Dye, in his jog around the bases, overruns Paul Konerko, the runner on first, and is called out. The final score should be Chicago 7, Detroit 5. True or False?

3. The Diamondbacks have Orlando Hudson on third and Justin Upton on first with the Mets infield playing shallow to make a play at the plate. Adam Dunn smashes a hot grounder right between the legs of Mets first baseman Carlos Delgado. The ball is deflected and Upton, running between first and second, intentionally kicks the ball as it gets near him. The umpires properly call Upton out but allow Hudson to score because the ball was deflected by Delgado. True or False?

4. Aramis Ramirez is on third base for the Cubs when Daryle Ward hits a high fly ball to Ryan Freel in the Reds outfield. Ramirez assumes a position several feet beyond the third-base bag and times his running start so that he is at full speed easily on the play, but the Reds appeal that Ramirez should be out for making an improper tag-up or retouch. The umpires uphold the appeal and Ramirez is called out. True or False?

5. The Twins have Adam Everett on first when Nick Punto hits an apparent triple. As Everett is circling the bases, he misses second. After he touches third, the Twins' third-base coach tells him to go back to second. Everett retouches third and starts for second when he sees Punto heading for third. Punto puts the brakes on and retreats to second and then on to first. Everett winds up safely at second. The Royals appeal that Everett cannot retreat to touch a missed base (second base) since he already touched third base. The umps disagree and correctly allow the play to stand. True or False?

6. The Marlins have Jeremy Hermida on first when Cody Ross hits a ground ball to Rockies' third baseman Garrett Atkins who throws to second, retiring Hermida. But Hermida continues to advance toward third base. The first baseman, Todd Helton, comes off the bag early to get the ball so he can nail Hermida (who was already called out) at third. The umpires correctly call Ross out because Hermida confused the defense by continuing to run after he had been called out. True or False?

7. The Yankees' Jason Giambi hits a speaker hanging over fair territory at Tropicana Field. The ball ricochets off the speaker and is caught by outfielder Carl Crawford. The umpires properly rule this to be a legal catch. True or False?

8. In the top of the fifth inning, Phillies manager Charlie Manuel makes a trip to the mound to settle down his pitcher Ryan Madson. Freddy Sanchez, the Pirates' next batter, gets a hit. This time Manuel sends his pitching coach out to calm Madson. Since the coach and not the manager went to the mound, the umpires correctly allow Madson to pitch to another batter. True or False?

9. Dodgers batter Juan Pierre taps a ground ball to Astros' first baseman Lance Berkman. Houston pitcher Roy Oswalt comes over to take the toss from Berkman, but contact occurs between Oswalt and Pierre as they both converge on first base. The umpire correctly rules obstruction on Oswalt since he was not fielding a ball in flight near him. True or False?

10. The Giants have Bengie Molina on first base with a 3-2 count on Rich Aurilia and one out. Aurilia checks his swing as the home plate umpire calls "Ball Four." Padres catcher Michael Barrett asks the plate ump to get help from the third-base umpire who reverses the call to "Strike Three," declaring Aurilia out. Meanwhile Molina, the runner from first, has started a slow trot to second and is tagged out by Padres shortstop Khalil Greene. Molina should not be called out because the home plate ump originally called "Ball Four" on Aurilia. True or False?

QUIZ 14

Answers on page 95

1. Two shortstops have won ten or more Gold Glove awards during their careers. Collect five points for each of these players you can identify.

2. Ty Cobb put together a 40-game hitting streak in 1911 and a 35-game skein in 1917 for the Detroit Tigers. Who is the only other batter to have two hitting streaks of 30 or more games during his career in the majors: Joe DiMaggio, George Brett, Pete Rose, or George Sisler?

3. In 1987, the New York Mets became the first team to have two players (Darryl Strawberry and Howard Johnson) with 30 or more homers and 30-plus stolen bases. The 1996 Colorado Rockies are the only other club to match this feat. Identify the two Colorado players to have 30 or more homers and stolen bases in 1996. Collect five points for each correct answer.

4. Which one of the following sluggers did not hit 100 home runs in both the American League and National League: Ellis Burks, George Hendrick, Dave Kingman, or Graig Nettles?

5. Who is the only player to hit 40 or more doubles in a season with four different clubs: Rogers Hornsby, Alfonso Soriano, Dick Allen, or Bill Buckner?

6. Four 300-game winners have won 20 games in a season for a last-place team. Which one of the following pitchers did not accomplish this feat for a cellar dweller: Nolan Ryan, Roger Clemens, Steve Carlton, Tom Seaver, or Phil Niekro?

7. Who is the only pitcher to hit two grand slams in one game: Bob Gibson, Rudy May, Tony Cloninger, or Wes Ferrell?

8. In 2006, David Ortiz became the 13th player in Boston Red Sox history to win an A.L. home run crown. Collect ten points if you can identify five of the other 12 Red Sox to win a HR title.

9. Since 1985, there have been three different league batting champions who wore uniform No. 51. Collect ten points if you can identify one of these hitting title winners.

10. The last major league team to have three 20-game winners on its pitching staff was the 1973 world champion Oakland A's. For ten points, correctly identify each of the three pitchers on that Oakland staff.

DID YOU KNOW ... that Rob Deer, Mark McGwire, and Ruben Rivera are the only players to hit 20 or more homers in a season while batting below .200? Deer slugged 25 homers for the Tigers in 1991 while hitting .179. McGwire posted a .187 hitting mark for the Cardinals in 2001 when he clubbed 29 homers. In 1999, Rivera finished the year with 23 homers and a .195 BA for the Padres.

DID YOU KNOW . . . that Cesar Geronimo is the only player to be the 3,000th strikeout victim of two different big league pitchers? On July 17, 1974, he was Bob Gibson's 3,000th K-victim, and on July 4, 1980, he was Nolan Ryan's.

ANSWERS TO QUIZ 1 *From page 9*

1. The ten players with 3,000 lifetime hits who finished their careers with a batting average below .300 include Carl Yastrzemski (.285), Eddie Murray (.287), Cal Ripken (.276), Robin Yount (.285), Dave Winfield (.283), Craig Biggio (.281), Rickey Henderson (.279), Lou Brock (.293), Rafael Palmeiro (.288), and Al Kaline (.297).

2. Besides Tim McCarver, the only other catcher to lead the league in triples was Carlton Fisk. In 1972, Fisk tied for the American League lead in triples with Joe Rudi of the Oakland A's.

3. The only pitcher to win a World Series game for three different teams during his career is Curt Schilling, who received credit for a victory in the 1993 World Series with the Philadelphia Phillies, in the 2001 Fall Classic with the Arizona Diamondbacks, and in the 2004 and 2007 Series with the Boston Red Sox.

4. Reggie Jackson of the A's and Brewers' slugger George Scott tied for the 1975 American League home run crown with 32. In 1980, Jackson of the Yankees and Milwaukee's Ben Oglivie tied for the HR leadership with 41. In 1982, Jackson clubbed 39 homers for the Angels to tie Gorman Thomas of the Brewers for the A.L. lead in home runs.

5. The only pitcher in major league history to win Rookie of the Year honors and a Cy Young and MVP award is Don Newcombe, who was the National League's top rookie in 1949 and captured the N.L. MVP and Cy Young awards with the Dodgers in 1956.

6. Besides Ty Cobb and Rickey Henderson,

Puzzle 1 Solution
from page 11

the five other players to score more than 2,000 career runs in the major leagues are Barry Bonds (2,227), Hank Aaron (2,174), Babe Ruth (2,174), Pete Rose (2,165), and Willie Mays (2,062).

7. Joe Jackson's .356 lifetime batting average is the highest among players with 5,000 or more plate appearances who never won a league batting title. Jackson had three second-place finishes, two third-place, and three fourth-place finishes among the top hitters for the American League batting championship during his career.

8. Besides Eddie Murray, the only other player to hit 500 or more career homers while ending his career with a slugging percentage below .500 is Reggie Jackson, who totaled 563 homers with a .490 slugging average.

9. Babe Ruth is the only player in big league history with 2,000 or more hits, walks, runs, and RBIs. Ruth finished his career with 2,873 hits, 2,174 runs, 2,217 RBIs and 2,062 walks.

10. Todd Helton is the only player to have consecutive seasons collecting 100 or more extra-base hits. In 2000, Helton amassed 103 extra-base hits (59 doubles, two triples, 42 home runs) and in 2001, he totaled 105 extra-base hits (54 doubles, two triples, 49 home runs) for the Colorado Rockies.

From the Disabled List to the Detention Center

Early in the 1996 season, Colorado Rockies outfielder Larry Walker was on the disabled list with a broken collarbone he suffered when crashing into a wall in an attempt to catch a ball. During his time on the DL, Walker spent time in the Rockies bullpen to get a reliever's perspective. "It's boring," he said. "They don't move. They flick sunflower seeds to keep themselves excited. You just sit in a chair and stare straight ahead like a mannequin. You feel like a kid in detention."

ANSWERS TO QUIZ 2

From page 12

1. The 23 players to hit 30 or more home runs during their rookie season in the majors:

Year	Player, Team	HR
1987	Mark McGwire, Oakland A's	49
1930	Wally Berger, Boston Braves	38
1956	Frank Robinson, Cincinnati Reds	38
1950	Al Rosen, Cleveland Indians	37
2001	Albert Pujols, St. Louis Cardinals	37
1934	Hal Trosky, Cleveland Indians	35
1937	Rudy York, Detroit Tigers	35
1983	Ron Kittle, Chicago White Sox	35
1993	Mike Piazza, Los Angeles Dodgers	35
1950	Walt Dropo, Boston Red Sox	34
2007	Ryan Braun, Milwaukee Brewers	34
1963	Jimmie Hall, Minnesota Twins	33
1971	Earl Williams, Atlanta Braves	33
1986	Jose Canseco, Oakland A's	33
1964	Tony Oliva, Minnesota Twins	32
1987	Matt Nokes, Detroit Tigers	32
1939	Ted Williams, Boston Red Sox	31
1964	Jim Ray Hart, San Francisco Giants	31
1993	Tim Salmon, California Angels	31
1959	Bobby Allison, Washington Senators	30
1971	Willie Montanez, Philadelphia Phillies	30
1986	Pete Incaviglia, Texas Rangers	30
1997	Nomar Garciaparra, Boston Red Sox	30

2. The only two managers to win a World Series in both the American League and National League are Sparky Anderson and Tony LaRussa. Anderson led the Cincinnati Reds to world championships in 1975 and 1976 in the N.L. and the A.L. Detroit Tigers to a World Series victory in 1984. LaRussa accomplished the feat in the A.L. with the Oakland A's in 1989 and in the N.L. with the Cardinals in 2006.

3. Tris Speaker, who is the career leader in two-base hits with 792, holds the record for most 40-double seasons in his career with ten.

4. Hall of Famer Lloyd Waner totaled the fewest extra-base hits (25) in a season for a player who had 200 or more safeties in one year. In his rookie season with the Pirates in 1927, Waner recorded 223 hits, including 17 doubles, six triples, two home runs, and 198 singles.

5. Randy Johnson is credited with the most strikeouts by a relief pitcher with 16, on July 19, 2001. The contest began on July 18, but due to a power failure at Qualcomm Stadium in San Diego, the game was suspended and resumed in the second inning on July 19. Johnson relieved for starter Curt Schilling and pitched the third through ninth innings, picking up 16 strikeouts and a victory.

6. The six players to win a batting title with two different clubs are Nap Lajoie (A's and Indians), Rogers Hornsby (Cardinals and Braves), Lefty O'Doul (Phillies and Dodgers), Jimmie Foxx (A's and Red Sox), Ernie Lombardi (Reds and Braves), and Bill Madlock (Cubs and Pirates).

7. The only player to lead his league in hits for three different teams is Paul Molitor who topped the American League in hits with the Milwaukee Brewers in 1991, with the Toronto Blue Jays in 1993, and with the Minnesota Twins in 1996.

8. Todd Zeile holds the major league record for hitting a home run with the most different clubs (11) during his career. In his 16 seasons in the majors, Zeile homered for the Cardinals (75), Cubs (9), Phillies (20), Orioles (5), Dodgers (38), Marlins (6), Rangers (30), Mets (41), Rockies (18), Yankees (6), and Expos (5).

9. Albert Belle is the only player to club 50 or more doubles and home runs in the same season when he accomplished the feat for the Cleveland Indians in 1995 with 52 doubles and 50 homers.

10. The three relievers since 1969 who are credited with a no-hitter and led their league in saves are Dennis Eckersley, Dave Righetti, and Derek Lowe. Eckersley paced the A.L.

in saves in 1988 and 1992 for the A's and pitched a no-hitter for Cleveland on May 30, 1977. Righetti worked a hitless game for the Yankees on July 4, 1983, and topped the A.L. in saves for New York in 1986. Lowe was the A.L. saves leader in 2000 with the Red Sox and completed a no-hitter with Boston on April 27, 2002.

ANSWERS TO RULES CHALLENGE 1 *From page 13*

1. True. (7.09-m) — It is interference by a batter or a runner when: A fair ball touches the runner in fair territory before touching a fielder. If a fair ball goes through, or by, an infielder, and touches a runner immediately behind him, or touches the runner after having been deflected by a fielder, the umpire shall not declare the runner out for being touched by a batted ball. In making such a decision the umpire must be convinced that the ball passed through, or by, the fielder, and that no other infielder had the chance to make a play on the ball. If, in the judgment of the umpire, the runner deliberately and intentionally kicks such a batted ball on which the infielder has missed a play, then the runner shall be called out for interference.

2. True. (7.11) — The players, coaches or any member of an offensive team shall vacate any space (including both dugouts) needed by a fielder who is attempting to field a batted or thrown ball.

3. False. Quentin should be awarded two bases. (6.09-g) — Any bounding fair ball is deflected by the fielder into the stands, or over or under a fence on fair or foul territory, in which case the batter and all runners shall be entitled to advance two bases. (7.05-f) — All runners shall advance two bases without liability if a fair ball bounces or is deflected into the stands outside the first or third base foul lines; or if it goes through or under a field fence, or through or under shrubbery or vines on the fence; or if it sticks in such a fence, scoreboard, shrubbery, or vines.

4. False. (6.06-a) — A batter is out for illegal action when he hits a ball with one or both feet on the ground entirely outside the batter's box.

5. False. Umpires try to call time when they can prevent the pitch. In this case, there is no actual interference. (3.16) — When there is spectator interference with any thrown or batted ball, the ball shall be dead at the moment of interference and the umpire shall impose such penalties as in his opinion will nullify the act of interference.

6. False. The runner is out for coach's interference if (7.09-i) — In the judgment of the umpire, the base coach at third base, or first base, by touching or holding the runner, physically assists him in returning to or leaving third base or first base.

7. False. (7.08c-1) — If the impact of a runner breaks a base loose from its position, no play can be made on the runner if he had reached the base safely.

8. True. (2.00) — A bunt is a batted ball not swung at, but intentionally met with the bat and tapped slowly within the field.

9. True. (10.05-e) — A base hit shall be scored when a fair ball which has not been touched by a fielder touches a runner or an umpire. EXCEPTION: Do not score a hit when a runner is called out for having been touched by an Infield Fly.

10. True. (2.00) — Obstruction is the act of a fielder who, while not in possession of the ball and not in the act of fielding the ball, impedes the progress of any runner.

ANSWERS TO QUIZ 3   *From page 15*

1. The four players who have hit 200 or more career home runs in both the American League and the National League are Frank Robinson, Mark McGwire, Fred McGriff, and Ken Griffey, Jr.

2. Outfielder Owen Wilson of the Pittsburgh Pirates set a major league record by hitting 36 triples in 1912. During the 1912 season, Wilson hit five triples in April, six in May, six in June, nine in July, seven in August, two in September, and one in October.

3. Besides George Sisler, Al Oliver, Bill Buckner, and Vladimir Guerrero, the only other player to produce a 200-hit season in both leagues is Steve Sax, who totaled 210 hits for the Dodgers in the National League in 1986 and had 205 safeties for the Yankees in the A.L. in 1989.

Dennis Eckersley

4. Hall of Famer Dave Winfield is the only major league player to collect 1,000 or more career hits in both the American League and National League. Among his lifetime total of 3,110 hits, 1,134 were achieved in the N.L. and 1,976 in the A.L.

5. The nine pitchers to win a Cy Young and MVP award in the same season are Don Newcombe, Dodgers (1956), Sandy Koufax, Dodgers (1963), Denny McLain, Tigers (1968), Bob Gibson, Cardinals (1968), Vida Blue, A's (1971), Rollie Fingers, Brewers (1981), Willie Hernandez, Tigers (1984), Roger Clemens, Red Sox (1986), and Dennis Eckersley, A's (1992).

6. The New York Yankee player to be named the American League MVP in 1942 over Triple Crown winner Ted Williams of the Red Sox was second baseman Joe Gordon, who hit .322 with 18 homers and 103 RBI.

7. Sammy Sosa holds the record for most home runs hit in one month with 20. In June 1998, Sosa clubbed 20 of his season total 65 home runs. The previous mark was 18 by Rudy York of the Tigers in August 1937.

8. Ty Cobb was the youngest player to reach the 3,000-hit plateau at the age of 34 years, 245 days. Robin Yount was 36 years, 358 days. Hank Aaron reached the milestone at 36 years, 101 days while Pete Rose did it at age 37 years, 21 days.

9. The following players collected 200 or more hits and 50-plus stolen bases in the same season: Ty Cobb

(1909–1912, 1915–1917), Tris Speaker (1912), Sam Rice (1920), George Sisler (1922), Snuffy Stirnweiss (1944), Willie Wilson (1980), Kenny Lofton (1996), and Ichiro Suzuki (2001) in the American League. In the N.L. it was accomplished by Honus Wagner (1908), Max Carey (1922), Maury Wills (1962), Lou Brock (1967, 1970–1971), Willie McGee (1985), Tony Gwynn (1985), Lance Johnson (1996), Craig Biggio (1998), Juan Pierre (2003, 2006), Hanley Ramirez (2007), and Jose Reyes (2008).

10. The 13 players to hit four home runs in one game in the major leagues since 1900 include Chuck Klein, Gil Hodges, Joe Adcock, Willie Mays, Mike Schmidt, Bob Horner, Mark Whiten, and Shawn Green in the National League, and Lou Gehrig, Pat Seerey, Rocky Colavito, Mark Cameron, and Carlos Delgado in the A.L.

ANSWERS TO PHOTO QUIZ 1

From page 16

A — Hank Aaron (1)	**K** — Carl Yastrzemski (27)
B — Al Simmons (22)	**L** — Carl Hubbell (14)
C — Cy Young (28)	**M** — Don Drysdale (9)
D — Gary Sheffield (21)	**N** — Larry Bowa (6)
E — Joe Jackson (15)	**O** — Reggie Jackson (16)
F — Johnny Bench (3)	**P** — Grover Alexander (2)
G — Rick Sutcliffe (25)	**Q** — Warren Spahn (24)
H — Bob Feller (10)	**R** — Gil Hodges (13)
I — Chipper Jones (17)	**S** — Pete Rose (20)
J — Hank Greenberg (12)	**T** — Yogi Berra (4)

ANSWERS TO QUIZ 4   *From page 18*

1. The 1974 American League MVP award winner was Texas Rangers' outfielder Jeff Burroughs, who hit .301 with 25 home runs and a league-leading 118 RBIs.

2. Besides Barry Bonds, the ten other players to win consecutive league MVP honors include Jimmie Foxx (1932–1933), Hal Newhouser (1944–1945), Yogi Berra (1954–1955),

Mickey Mantle (1956–1957), Roger Maris (1960–1961), and Frank Thomas (1993–1994) in the American League, with Ernie Banks (1958–1959), Joe Morgan (1975–1976), Mike Schmidt (1980–1981), and Dale Murphy (1982–1983) accomplishing the feat in the N.L.

3. The four players to end their careers with 500 or more homers and 3,000-plus hits are Hank Aaron, Willie Mays, Eddie Murray, and Rafael Palmeiro.

4. Walter Johnson holds the major league record for most career shutouts with 110. During his 21 years with the Washington Senators, Johnson won 417 games. He topped the A.L. in shutouts seven times and tossed at least one shutout in 21 consecutive seasons (1907–1927).

5. Among pitchers with 300 or more lifetime wins, Tom Glavine threw the fewest shutouts with 25. Lefty Grove and Greg Maddux had 35 while Tim Keefe totaled 39.

6. The four closers to be a league saves leader for both an A.L. and N.L. club since 1969 are Rollie Fingers (Brewers in the A.L. and Padres), Mike Marshall (Twins, Expos, Dodgers), Lee Smith (Orioles, Cubs, Cardinals), and Randy Myers (Orioles and Cubs).

7. Dodgers speedster Maury Wills was the first player since 1900 to steal 100 or more bases in a single season when he swiped 104 in 1962.

8. Since 1900, the nine pitchers to have multiple 300-strikeout seasons in the major leagues are Rube Waddell (1903–1904), Walter Johnson (1910, 1912), Sandy Koufax (1963, 1965–1966), Sam McDowell (1965, 1970), Nolan Ryan (1972–1974, 1976–1977, 1989), J. R. Richard (1978–1979), Randy Johnson (1993, 1998–2002), Curt Schilling (1997–1998, 2002), and Pedro Martinez (1997, 1999).

9. Besides Frank McCormick, Rogers Hornsby, Ginger Beaumont, Ty Cobb, Tony Oliva, and Ichiro Suzuki, the only other batter to lead his league in hits for three consecutive seasons was Kirby Puckett. Puckett paced the A.L. in hits from 1987 through 1989 with the Minnesota Twins.

10. Babe Ruth and Jimmie Foxx are the only two players to win a batting title and lead the league in strikeouts in the same season. In 1924, Ruth led the A.L. with 46 homers and 81 strikeouts with the Yankees, and in 1933, Foxx topped the A.L. with 48 homers and 93 whiffs with the A's.

Name That Award Winner
From page 19

A. Frank Thomas won the A.L. MVP in 1993–1994, clubbed more than 500 lifetime home runs, and has not appeared in a World Series. He was on the 2005 White Sox World Series team but did not appear in the post-season due to injury. Thomas played tight end and signed a football scholarship to Auburn University.

B. Denny McLain won two Cy Young Awards with the Detroit Tigers in 1968–1969 and posted a career 131-91 won-lost record in the majors. He was first signed by the White Sox in 1962 as an amateur free agent but pitched in the majors for the Tigers, Washington Senators, Oakland A's, and Atlanta Braves.

C. In 1990, Sandy Alomar, Jr., joined Carlton Fisk as the only catchers to win Rookie of the Year honors and a Gold Glove award in the same season. He won the 1997 All-Star game MVP Award with a game-winning two-run homer. Alomar posted a 30-game hitting streak for the Indians in 1997, becoming only the second catcher to accomplish the feat (Benito Santiago, 34-game streak in 1987).

D. Reggie Jackson won the World Series MVP in 1973 with the Oakland A's and in 1977 with the Yankees. During his career, he clubbed 563 homers, drove in 1,702 runs, stole 228 bases, and fanned 2,597 times while batting .262.

Puzzle 2 Solution
from page 20

ANSWERS TO QUIZ 5 *From page 22*

1. The player with the lowest batting average to win a league Most Valuable Player award (through 2007) was Cardinals' shortstop Marty Marion, who hit .267 when he captured the N.L. MVP honor in 1944.

2. The five Rookie of the Year award winners who went on to collect 3,000 or more hits during their major league careers are Willie Mays (3,283), Pete Rose (4,256), Rod Carew (3,053), Eddie Murray (3,255), and Cal Ripken, Jr. (3,184).

3. During his rookie season in 1985, left-hander Tom Browning of the Cincinnati Reds posted a 20-9 won-lost record but did not win the National League Rookie of the Year award. The honor went to Cardinals' outfielder Vince Coleman, who hit .267 with 110 stolen bases and 107 runs scored.

4. Pete Rose holds the major league mark for most 200-hit seasons with ten. Stan Musial had six, Wade Boggs seven, and Ty Cobb nine.

5. The five batters who totaled more than 3,500 career hits in the major leagues are Pete Rose (4,256), Ty Cobb (4,189), Hank Aaron (3,771), Stan Musial (3,630), and Tris Speaker (3,514).

6. In Game 6 of the 1986 World Series between the Mets and Red Sox, the winning run was scored by New York's Ray Knight, after Mookie Wilson hit a ground ball to Boston first baseman Bill Buckner, whose error allowed the run to score.

7. Gene Mauch managed 27 years in the major leagues with the Philadelphia Phillies, Montreal Expos, Minnesota Twins, and California Angels, winning 1,902 games and two division titles — but he never won a pennant or World Series title.

8. Besides Alex Rodriguez, the only other player in the majors to hit 40 or more homers in a season with three different teams is Jim Thome. Rodriguez did it with the Mariners,

Rangers, and Yankees while Thome accomplished the feat with the Indians, Phillies, and White Sox.

9. Willie Mays drove in 1,903 runs during his career without ever leading the league in that category. Mays finished second in RBIs in the N.L. two times and third, three times.

10. Rod Carew of the Angels collected his 3,000th big league hit on August 4, 1985, the same day Tom Seaver of the White Sox won his 300th game. Carew's milestone hit was a single off Twins' pitcher Frank Viola in Anaheim, and Seaver pitched a complete-game, 4-1 win over the Yankees in New York.

ANSWERS TO RULES CHALLENGE 2 *From page 23*

1. False. Cesar Izturis could not advance home because Ryan Ludwick was an improper batter. (6.07-b) — When an improper batter becomes a runner or is put out, and the defensive team appeals to the umpire before the first pitch to the next batter of either team, or before any play or attempted play, the umpire shall (1) declare the proper batter out; and (2) nullify any advance or score made because of a ball batted by the improper batter or because of the improper batter's advance to first base on a hit, an error, a base on balls, a hit batter or otherwise. NOTE: If a runner advances while the improper batter is at bat, on a stolen base, balk, wild pitch, or passed ball, such advance is legal.

2. False. Izturis should be allowed to stay on second base. His advance on the wild pitch was legal.

3. False. Even though the interference was accidental, a "kick" is considered intentional and the extra-base advance is nullified. Carlos Lee should be returned to third. (3.15) — No person shall be allowed on the playing field during a game except players and coaches in uniform, managers, news photographers authorized by the home team, umpires, officers of the law in uniform, and watchmen or other employees of the home club. In case of unintentional interference with play by any person herein authorized to be on the playing field (except members of the offensive team participating in the game, or a coach in the coach's box, or an umpire), the ball is alive and in play. If the interference is intentional, the ball shall be dead at the moment of the interference and the umpire shall impose such penalties as in his opinion will nullify the act of interference. Rule 3.15 Comment: The question of intentional or unintentional interference shall be decided on the basis of the person's action. For example: a bat boy, ball attendant, policeman, etc., who tries to avoid being touched by a thrown or batted ball but still is touched by the ball would be involved in unintentional interference. If, however, he kicks the ball or picks it up or pushes it, that is considered intentional interference, regardless of what his thought may have been.

4. False. Ian Kinsler should be sent to third. A runner is awarded two bases from the last base he legally occupied in such situations. (7.05-g) — Each runner including the batter-runner may, without liability to be put out, advance two bases when, with no spectators on the playing field, a thrown ball goes into the stands, or into a bench (whether or not the ball rebounds into the field), or over or under or through a field fence, or on a slanting part of the screen above the backstop, or remains in the meshes of a wire screen protecting spectators. In all other cases the umpire shall be governed by the position of the runners at the time the wild throw was made. Rule 7.05-g Comment: In certain circumstances it is impossible to award a runner two bases. Example: Runner on first. Batter hits fly to short right. Runner holds up between first and second and batter comes around first and pulls up behind him. Ball falls safely. Outfielder, in throwing to first, throws ball into stands.

5. True. The ball is alive and in play since it has passed an infielder. (6.08-d) — The batter becomes a runner and is entitled to first base without liability to be put out (provided he advances to and touches first base) when — A fair ball touches an umpire or a runner on fair territory before touching a fielder. If a fair ball touches an umpire after having passed a fielder other than the pitcher, or having touched a fielder, including the pitcher, the ball is in play.

6. False. Victor Martinez should be ruled out at second base. The ejection does not take effect until no further action is possible. (9.01-d) — Each umpire has authority to disqualify any player, coach, manager, or substitute for objecting to decisions or for unsportsmanlike conduct or language, and to eject such disqualified person from the playing field. If an umpire disqualifies a player while a play is in progress, the disqualification shall not take effect until no further action is possible in that play.

7. True. (7.08-d) — Any runner is out when — He fails to retouch his base after a fair or foul ball is legally caught before he, or his base, is tagged by a fielder. He shall not be called out for failure to retouch his base after the first following pitch, or any play or attempted play. This is an appeal play; Rule 7.08-d Comment: Runners need not "tag up" on a foul tip. They may steal on a foul tip. If a so-called tip is not caught, it becomes an ordinary foul. Runners then return to their bases.

8. False. An injury visit is not counted as a trip. In this case, manager Bud Black was charged with only one trip. (8.06-a) — A professional league shall adopt the following rule pertaining to the visit of the manager or coach to the pitcher: This rule limits the number of trips a manager or coach may make to any one pitcher in any one inning.

9. False. The game is declared a suspended contest. (4.12-a-5) — (a) A game shall become a suspended game that must be completed at a future date if the game is terminated for any of the following reasons: (1) A curfew imposed by law; (2) A time limit permissible under league rules; (3) Light failure or malfunction of a mechanical field device under control of the home club; (4) Darkness, when a law prevents the lights from being turned on; (5) Weather, if a regulation game is called while an inning is in progress and before the inning is completed, and the visiting team has scored one or more runs to take the lead, and the home team has not retaken the lead; or (6) It is a regulation game that is called with the score tied.

10. True. A batter cannot intentionally deflect either a foul or fair ball. (6.05-i) — A batter is out when after hitting or bunting a foul ball, he intentionally deflects the course of the ball in any manner while running to first base. The ball is dead and no runners may advance.

ANSWERS TO QUIZ 6 *From page 25*

1. Among the 24 major league players with 10,000 or more career at-bats, Rabbit Maranville posted the lowest batting average with a .258 mark. Maranville played 23 seasons with 10,078 at-bats and 2,605 hits.

2. The eight left-handed pitchers with 2,500 or more career strikeouts in the majors include Randy Johnson, Steve Carlton, Mickey Lolich, Frank Tanana, Chuck Finley, Tom Glavine, Warren Spahn, and Jerry Koosman.

3. Billy Williams won the 1961 National League Rookie of the Year award with the Chicago Cubs but never won league MVP honors. Dick Allen was the N.L. Rookie of the Year in 1964 and the A.L. MVP in 1972. Thurman Munson captured A.L. rookie honors in 1970 and the MVP Award in 1976. Rod Carew was voted the A.L.'s top rookie in 1967 and the Most Valuable Player in 1977 while Orlando Cepeda won Rookie of the Year in the N.L. in 1958 and MVP in 1967.

4. Besides Walter Johnson and Grover Alexander, the only other pitcher since 1900 to lead his league in shutouts for three consecutive seasons is Roger Clemens, who paced the American League in scoreless games from 1990 through 1992 with the Boston Red Sox.

5. Listed in the accompanying chart are the 13 different pitchers who won 30 or more games in a season in the major leagues since 1900.

Year	Pitcher, Team	W-L	ERA
1904	Jack Chesbro, Highlanders	41-12	1.82
1908	Ed Walsh, White Sox	40-15	1.42
1908	Christy Mathewson, Giants	37-11	1.43
1913	Walter Johnson, Senators	36-7	1.14
1904	Joe McGinnity, Giants	35-8	1.61

Year	Pitcher, Team	W-L	ERA
1912	Joe Wood, Red Sox	34-5	1.91
1901	Cy Young, Red Sox	33-10	1.62
1904	Christy Mathewson, Giants	33-12	2.03
1912	Walter Johnson, Senators	33-12	1.39
1916	Grover Alexander, Phillies	33-12	1.55
1902	Cy Young, Red Sox	32-11	2.15
1903	Joe McGinnity, Giants	31-20	2.43
1905	Christy Mathewson, Giants	31-9	1.28
1910	Jack Coombs, A's	31-9	1.30
1915	Grover Alexander, Phillies	31-10	1.22
1920	Jim Bagby, Indians	31-12	2.89
1931	Lefty Grove, A's (left-hander)	31-4	2.06
1968	Denny McLain, Tigers	31-6	1.96
1903	Christy Mathewson, Giants	30-13	2.26
1917	Grover Alexander, Phillies	30-13	1.83
1934	Dizzy Dean, Cardinals	30-7	2.66

6. Since 1900, the six league batting champions whose last name begins with the letter "O" are Lefty O'Doul (1929, 1932), Tony Oliva (1964–1965, 1971), Al Oliver (1982), John Olerud (1993), Paul O'Neill (1994), and Magglio Ordonez (2007).

7. The five switch-hitters who have led the league in RBIs since 1956 include Mickey Mantle, Yankees (1956), Eddie Murray, Orioles (1981), Ruben Sierra, Rangers (1989), Howard Johnson, Mets (1991), and Lance Berkman, Astros (2002).

8. Besides Barry Bonds, the only other player to have a 50-steal season and a 50-homer campaign during his major league career is Brady Anderson. Anderson stole 53 bases in 1992 and clubbed 50 homers in 1996 for the Baltimore Orioles. Bonds hit 73 homers for the Giants in 2001 and swiped 52 bases for the Pirates in 1990.

9. In the 1993 World Series, Joe Carter belted his walk-off homer in Game 6 to clinch the world championship for the Toronto Blue Jays against Phillies' pitcher Mitch Williams.

10. Garret Anderson never hit 50 or more doubles in back-to-back seasons. Anderson had his only 50-double campaign in 2002 when he totaled 56 two-baggers for the Angels.

ANSWERS TO QUIZ 7

From page 28

1. False. Mickey Mantle and Eddie Murray are the only two switch-hitters with 500 or more career homers. Mantle finished his career with 536 and Murray with 504.

2. False. Hank Aaron and Barry Bonds are the only two players with 600 or more homers and doubles during their careers. Aaron totaled 755 homers and 624 doubles while Bonds finished with 762 HR and 601 doubles.

3. True. During Ted Williams' Triple Crown–winning seasons (1942, 1947), he did not win the American League MVP award. In 1942, Williams lost the MVP to Yankees' second baseman Joe Gordon and in 1947 to Yankee outfielder Joe DiMaggio.

4. True. Babe Ruth hit 20 or more homers in a season 16 times during his career as an outfielder with the Red Sox and Yankees, and as a pitcher he won 23 games in 1916 and 24 in 1917 with Boston.

5. False. Red Sox right-hander Mike Torrez was the pitcher when Bucky Dent hit his home run in the 1978 play-off game to decide the A.L. East division crown.

6. True. Darin Erstad is the only player to win a Gold Glove award at different positions. Erstad won a Gold Glove as a first baseman in 2004 and as a center fielder in 2000 and 2002 with the Angels.

7. False. Babe Ruth hit three homers in one World Series game twice during his career. Ruth did it in Game 4 of the 1926 Series against the Cardinals and in Game 4 of the 1928 Fall Classic against the Cardinals. Jackson did it in Game 6 of the 1977 World Series against the Dodgers.

**Puzzle 3 Solution
from page 26**

75

8. True. Jim Palmer never surrendered a grand slam in the 3,948 innings he pitched in the major leagues.

9. False. The first pitcher to win the Cy Young Award in both leagues was Gaylord Perry, who captured the honor in the American League in 1972 for the Indians and in the National League in 1978 with the Padres.

10. True. Tom Seaver's final big league victory came on August 18, 1986, when he hurled 8.2 innings for the Red Sox in a 3-1 Boston win over the Minnesota Twins.

11. False. Joining Bobby and Barry Bonds as the only father/son duo to club 30 homers in a major league season are Cecil and Prince Fielder, and Felipe and Moises Alou.

12. True. At age 20 years, 269 days, Tony Conigliaro won the A.L. home run title with the Boston Red Sox in 1965.

13. True. Willie Stargell of the Pirates hit the most home runs during the 1970s (1970–1979) with 296, followed by Reggie Jackson (292) and Johnny Bench (290).

14. True. Sandy Koufax won the Cy Young Award in 1963, 1965, and 1966 with the Dodgers to become the first pitcher to capture the honor three times.

15. True. The Yankees and A's are the only major league franchises to win at least three World Series titles in a row. The Yankees did it from 1936 to 1939, 1949 to 1953, and 1998 to 2000. The A's did it from 1972 to 1974.

16. False. Ichiro Suzuki set a new single-season hit mark in 2004 with 262 hits for the Seattle Mariners.

17. False. Rickey Henderson and Vince Coleman are the only players to steal 100 or more bases in a season three times. Henderson did it in 1980 (100), 1982 (130), and 1983 (108) for the A's while Coleman accomplished the feat with the Cardinals in 1985 (110), 1986 (107), and 1987 (109).

18. True. Oakland pitcher Dave Stewart was the last major league pitcher to win 20 or more games in four consecutive seasons when he did it from 1987 through 1990.

19. False. The first relief pitcher to save 40 or more games in a season was Dan Quisenberry of the Kansas City Royals when he recorded 45 saves in 1983.

20. True. Pete Rose is the all-time record holder for most career at-bats with 14,053.

ANSWERS TO
RULES CHALLENGE 3 *From page 30*

1. True. The balk by Beckett should be nullified. (4.06-a-3) — No manager, player, substitute, coach, trainer, or bat-boy shall at any time, whether from the bench, the coach's box, or on the playing field, or elsewhere — call "Time," or employ any other word or phrase or commit any act while the ball is alive and in play for the obvious purpose of trying to make the pitcher commit a balk.

2. False. Pence's run does not count since Berkman was the third out of the inning. (4.09-a) — One run shall be scored each time a runner legally advances to and touches first, second, third, and home base before three men are put out to end the inning. EXCEPTION: A run is not scored if the runner advances to home base during a play in which the third out is made (1) by the batter-runner before he touches first base; (2) by any runner being forced out; or (3) by a preceding runner who is declared out because he failed to touch one of the bases.

3. False. Because the ball deflected off Inge's chest protector before he secured the ball in his mitt, it is ruled a foul ball. (6.05-b) — A batter is out when a third strike is legally caught by the catcher. Rule 6.05-b Comment: "Legally caught" means in the catcher's glove before the ball touches the ground. It is not legal if the ball lodges in his clothing or paraphernalia; or if it touches the umpire and is caught by the catcher on the rebound. If a foul-tip first strikes the catcher's glove and then goes on through and is caught by both hands against his body or protector, before the ball touches the ground, it is a strike, and if third strike, batter is out. If smothered against his body or protector, it is a catch provided the ball struck the catcher's glove or hand first.

4. False. Hawpe should not be ruled out on the play. (6.05-h) — If a batted ball strikes a batting helmet or any other object foreign to the natural ground while on foul territory, it is a foul ball and the ball is dead. If, in the umpire's judgment, there is intent on the part of a base runner to interfere with a batted or thrown ball by dropping the helmet or throwing it at the ball, then the runner would be out, the ball dead, and runners would return to the last base legally touched.

5. True. Overbay's contact with the bag is all that is needed to record the out. (2.00 Tag) — A tag is the action of a fielder in touching a base with his body while holding the ball securely and firmly in his hand or glove; or touching a runner with the ball, or with his hand or glove holding the ball, while holding the ball securely and firmly in his hand or glove.

6. False. According to rule (5.09-b) — The ball becomes dead and runners advance one base, or return to their bases, without liability to be put out when the plate umpire interferes with the catcher's throw; runners may not advance. NOTE: The interference shall be disregarded if the catcher's throw retires the runner.

7. True. According to rule (4.15-c) — A game may be forfeited to the opposing team when a team refuses to continue play during a game unless the game has been suspended or terminated by the umpire.

8. False. Jones' helmet falling off (unintentionally) during a play is not interference if a ball strikes the helmet. (6.05-h) — If a batted ball strikes a batting helmet or any other object foreign to the natural ground while on foul territory, it is a foul ball and the ball is dead. If, in the umpire's judgment, there is intent on the part of a base runner to interfere with a batted or thrown ball by dropping the helmet or throwing it at the ball, then the runner would be out, the ball dead, and runners would return to last base legally touched.

9. False. Soriano scores. (6.05-n) — With two out, a runner on third base, and two strikes on the batter, the runner attempts to steal home base on a legal pitch and the ball touches the runner in the batter's strike zone. The umpire shall call "Strike Three," the batter is out and the run shall not count; before two are out, the umpire shall call "Strike Three," the ball is dead, and the run counts.

10. True. Lee is called out on strikes and Soriano's run does not count. (6.05-n) — refer to the rule in question 9.

ANSWERS TO PHOTO QUIZ 2

From page 32

A — Al Kaline (12)

B — Carlton Fisk (6)

C — Willie Stargell (21)

D — Rich Gossage (7)

E — H. Killebrew (13)

F — Denny McLain (17)

G — Steve Carlton (4)

H — Manny Ramirez (18)

I — Sammy Sosa (20)

J — Jeff Bagwell (1)

K — Randy Johnson (10)

L — Don Zimmer (24)

M — Tony Gwynn (8)

N — George Brett (3)

O — Tony La Russa (14)

P — Jim Hunter (9)

Q — Luis Tiant (23)

R — Rollie Fingers (5)

S — Ozzie Smith (19)

T — Don Sutton (22)

ANSWERS TO QUIZ 8 *From page 33*

1. Yogi Berra. I was the A.L. MVP in 1951, 1954, and 1955 while placing third in the voting in 1950, fourth in 1952, and second in 1953 and 1956. I clubbed the first pinch-hit homer in World Series history in Game 3 of the 1947 Series and hit 358 lifetime homers with the Yankees during my career.

2. Joe Morgan. My career began in 1963 with Houston and ended after the 1984 campaign with Oakland. During my 22 years in the majors, I captured five Gold Glove awards and two N.L. MVPs while being a member of the 1975–1976 Cincinnati Reds World Series teams. I stole 689 bases and hit 268 homers as a second baseman.

3. Stan Musial. I collected 3,630 career hits, including 475 home runs and seven N.L. batting titles. My most productive season was in 1948 when I led the N.L. with a .376 batting average, 131 RBIs, .450 on-base percentage, .702 slugging percentage, 135 runs, 230 hits, 46 doubles, 18 triples, and 103 extra-base hits while falling one homer shy (39) of winning the Triple Crown. I won the N.L. MVP award in 1943, 1946, and 1948.

4. Fred Lynn. I was the A.L. Rookie of the Year and MVP in 1975 with Boston, tying a league rookie mark with 47 doubles. I hit the only grand slam in All-Star game history in 1983 off Atlee Hammaker of the Giants.

5. David Cone. I won 194 games during my career with the Mets, Blue Jays, Royals, Yankees, and Red Sox, including a perfect game with the Yankees on July 18, 1999, against the Expos and a 19-strikeout performance for the Mets on October 6, 1991, against the Phillies. I was a 20-game winner for the Mets in 1988 (20-3) and for the Yankees in 1998 (20-7).

6. Ron Santo. I am the only third baseman to hit .300 or better with 30-plus homers and win a Gold Glove award in the same season more than once, accomplishing those feats in 1964, 1966, and 1967.

7. Dale Murphy. I won the N.L. MVP award in 1982 and 1983 with the Atlanta Braves and began my career as a catcher before becoming a Gold Glove–winning (1982–1986) center fielder. I won N.L. home run titles in 1984 and 1985.

8. Lee Smith. I saved 20 or more games in a season with the Cubs, Red Sox, Cardinals, Orioles, and Angels. My 478 career saves are third on the all-time list, and I surrendered a walk-off home run to Steve Garvey of the Padres in Game 4 of the 1984 NLCS when I was a closer with the Cubs.

9. Gabby Hartnett. I was the first National League catcher to win the MVP award (1935) since 1931. I clubbed 236 homers during my career spent mostly with the Cubs. I am the batter who hit the "Homer in the Gloamin'" on September 28, 1938, to help lead the Cubs to a pennant.

10. Bobby Bonds. My first major league hit was a grand slam off Dodgers pitcher John Purdin on June 25, 1968, at Candlestick Park in San Francisco. I was a member of the 30-homer, 30-steal club five times and hit 20-plus homers in a season for the Giants, Yankees, Angels, Rangers, and Indians.

ANSWERS TO QUIZ 9 *From page 35*

1. Among the 14 players with 600 or more lifetime doubles in major league history, Barry Bonds is the only member never to lead his league in two-base hits. Bonds hit 601 career doubles with a single-season high of 44 in 1998.

2. The two pitchers who have won three or more consecutive Cy Young Awards are Greg Maddux (1992–1995) and Randy Johnson (1999–2002).

3. Back-to-back MVP winners at the defensive positions include: Hal Newhouser (1944–1945), pitcher; Yogi Berra (1954–1955), catcher; Jimmie Foxx (1932–1933) and Frank Thomas (1993–1994), first base; Joe Morgan (1975–1976) second base; Mike Schmidt (1980–1981), third base; Ernie Banks (1958–1959), shortstop; Barry Bonds (1992–1993, 2001–2004), left field; Mickey Mantle (1956–1957), and Dale Murphy (1982–1983), center field; Roger Maris (1960–1961), right field.

4. The four Hall of Fame players whose last name begins with the letter "Y" are Carl Yastrzemski, Cy Young, Ross Youngs, and Robin Yount.

5. The nine teams Rickey Henderson played for during his career are the Oakland A's, New York Yankees, Toronto Blue Jays, San Diego Padres, Anaheim Angels, New York Mets, Seattle Mariners, Boston Red Sox, and Los Angeles Dodgers.

6. Bobby Cox holds the major league record for managers by being thrown out of a ball game 143 times through the 2008 season.

7. The four major league players who have struck out 2,000 or more times during their careers are Reggie Jackson (2,597), Sammy Sosa (2,306), Jim Thome (2,190), and Andres Galarraga (2,003).

8. Besides Jim Kaat, the ten other players to win ten or more consecutive Gold Glove awards include Brooks Robinson (16), Ozzie Smith (13), Greg Maddux (13), Willie Mays (12), Roberto Clemente (12), Keith Hernandez (11), Johnny Bench (10), Ken Griffey, Jr. (10), Ivan Rodriguez (10), and Andruw Jones (10).

9. The three players with the last name of Williams who have won a league batting title are Ted Williams (1941–1942, 1947–1948, 1957–1958) and Bernie Williams (1998) in the American League, and Billy Williams (1972) in the National League.

10. Wade Boggs is the only player to hit a home run for his 3,000th career hit when he connected off Chris Haney of the Indians on August 7, 1999, as a member of Tampa Bay.

ANSWERS TO RULES CHALLENGE 4 *From page 36*

1. True — (3.16) — When there is spectator interference with any thrown or batted ball, the ball shall be dead at the moment of interference and the umpire shall impose such penalties as in his opinion will nullify the act of interference. APPROVED RULING: If spectator interference clearly prevents a fielder from catching a fly ball, the umpire shall declare the batter out. Batter and runners shall be placed where in the umpire's judgment they would have been had the interference not occurred. Example: Runner on third base, one out, and a batter hits a fly ball deep to the outfield (fair or foul). Spectator clearly interferes with the outfielder attempting to catch the fly ball. Umpire calls the batter out for spectator interference. Ball is dead at the time of the call. Umpire decides that because of the distance the ball was hit, the runner on third base would have scored after the catch if the fielder had caught the ball which was interfered with, therefore the runner is permitted to score. This might not be the case if such fly ball was interfered with a short distance from home plate.

2. True — (6.06-c) — A batter is out for illegal action when he interferes with the catcher's fielding or throwing by stepping out of the batter's box or making any other movement that hinders the catcher's play at home base. Rule 6.06-c Comment: If the batter interferes with the catcher, the plate umpire shall call "interference." The batter is out and the ball dead. No player may advance on such interference (offensive interference), and all runners must return to the last base that was, in the judgment of the umpire, legally touched at the time of the interference.

3. False — (4.03) — When the ball is put in play at the start of or during a game, all fielders other than the catcher shall be on fair territory. (a) The catcher shall station himself directly back of the plate. He may leave his position at any time to catch a pitch or make a play except that when the batter is being given an intentional base on balls, the catcher must stand with both feet within the lines of the catcher's box until the ball leaves the pitcher's hand. PENALTY: Balk. (b) The pitcher, while in the act of delivering the ball to the batter, shall take his legal position. (c) Except the pitcher and the catcher, any fielder may station himself anywhere in fair territory.

4. True — (6.07 a-1) — A batter shall be called out, on appeal, when he fails to bat in his proper turn, and another batter completes a time at bat in his place. The proper batter may take his place in the batter's box at any time before the improper batter becomes a runner or is put out, and any balls and strikes shall be counted in the proper batter's time at bat.

5. False — (3.08 a-3) — If no announcement of a substitution is made, the substitute shall be considered as having entered the game when — if a fielder, he reaches the position usually occupied by the fielder he has replaced, and play commences.

6. False — (1.10) — The bat handle, for not more than 18 inches from its end, may be covered or treated with any material or substance to improve the grip. Any such material or substance, which extends past the 18-inch limitation, shall cause the bat to be removed from the game. NOTE: If the umpire discovers that the bat does not conform to the above rule until a time during or after which the bat has been used in play, it shall not be grounds for declaring the batter out, or ejected from the game.

7. False — (4.01-d) — As soon as the home team's batting order is handed to the umpire-in-chief, the umpires are in charge of the playing field and from that moment they shall have sole authority to determine when a game shall be called, suspended, or resumed on account of weather or the condition of the playing field. Rule 4.01 Comment: Obvious errors in the batting order, which are noticed by the umpire-in-chief before he calls "Play" for the start of the game, should

Puzzle 4 Solution
from page 40

be called to the attention of the manager or captain of the team in error, so the correction can be made before the game starts.

8. True — (1.01) — Baseball is a game between two teams of nine players each, under direction of a manager, played on an enclosed field in accordance with these rules, under jurisdiction of one or more umpires.

9. False — (1.15-c) — The umpire-in-chief shall cause a glove that violates Rules 1.15-a or 1.15-b to be removed from the game, either on his own initiative, at the recommendation of another umpire, or upon complaint of the opposing manager that the umpire-in-chief agrees has merit.

10. True — (6.07-b) — When an improper batter becomes a runner or is put out, and the defensive team appeals to the umpire, before the first pitch to the next batter of either team, or before any play or attempted play, the umpire shall (1) declare the proper batter out; and (2) nullify any advance or score made because of a ball batted by the improper batter or because of the improper batter's advance to first base on a hit, an error, a base on balls, a hit batter or otherwise. NOTE: If a runner advances, while the improper batter is at bat, on a stolen base, balk, wild pitch, or passed ball, such advance is legal.

Name That Pitcher Answers
From page 43

A. Ralph Terry. **B.** Mickey Lolich. **C.** Robin Roberts. **D.** Dave McNally. **E.** Grover Alexander.

ANSWERS TO QUIZ 10 *From page 42*

1. The two Yankee players who wore uniform No. 8 which was retired in their honor were Hall of Fame catchers Bill Dickey and Yogi Berra.

2. The seven Hall of Fame players who wore uniform No. 5 for most of their playing career include Joe DiMaggio, Hank Greenberg, Brooks Robinson, Johnny Bench, George Brett, Lou Boudreau, and Travis Jackson.

3. The two Hall of Fame pitchers to win three or more Cy Young Awards and who both wore uniform No. 32 are Steve Carlton and Sandy Koufax. Carlton won four Cy Young Awards (1972, 1977, 1980, 1982) and Koufax captured three (1963, 1965, 1966).

4. Al Kaline did not wear uniform No. 8 during his 22 seasons in the majors. He wore No. 6, which is retired by the Detroit Tigers in his honor.

5. True. During their long careers in the major leagues, Frank Robinson, Don Sutton, Lou Brock, and Mike Schmidt all wore uniform No. 20.

6. Nolan Ryan is the only other player besides Jackie Robinson to have his uniform number retired by three major league teams. Ryan's No. 30 was retired by the California Angels, and his No. 34 was retired by the Houston Astros and Texas Rangers.

7. When Barry Bonds and Mark McGwire hit 70-plus home runs they both wore uniform No. 25 the year they accomplished the feat. McGwire hit 70 homers in 1998 with the Cardinals, and Bonds clubbed 73 in 2001 with the Giants.

**Puzzle 5 Solution
from page 44**

8. The correct uniform numbers for the following players are Ernie Banks (14), Dave Winfield (31), Jim Palmer (22), Bob Gibson (45), and Bob Feller (19).

9. Chicago White Sox outfielder Carlos May wore his birthdate on the back of his uniform in the early 1970s. Born May 17, 1948, he wore No. 17 and often had his name on the back of his jersey.

10. The number worn by midget Eddie Gaedel of the St. Louis Browns on August 19, 1951, in his lone major league appearance was one-eighth (1/8).

ANSWERS TO
RULES CHALLENGE 5 *From page 46*

1. False. If the batter or his clothing is touched while in a legal batting position, he is awarded first base. (2.00) — The PERSON of a player or an umpire is any part of his body, his clothing, or his equipment. (6.08-b) — The batter becomes a runner and is entitled to first base without liability to be put out (provided he advances to and touches first base) when he is touched by a pitched ball which he is not attempting to hit unless (1) the ball is in the strike zone when it touches the batter, or (2) the batter makes no attempt to avoid being touched by the ball. If the ball is in the strike zone when it touches the batter, it shall be called a strike, whether or not the batter tries to avoid the ball. If the ball is outside the strike zone when it touches the batter, it shall be called a ball if he makes no attempt to avoid being touched.

2. False. When a batter is touched by a pitched ball that does not entitle him to first base, the ball is dead and no runner may advance. — (2.00, 6.08-b).

3. False. A runner may not return to touch home plate after another runner scores. (7.10-b) — Any runner shall be called out, on appeal, when with the ball in play, while advancing or returning to a base, he fails to touch each base in order before he, or a missed base, is tagged. APPROVED RULING: (1) No runner may return to touch a missed base after a following runner has scored. (2) When the ball is dead, no runner may return to touch a missed base or one he has left after he has advanced to and touched a base beyond the missed base.

4. True. If a batter hits a ball fair or foul while out of the batter's box, he shall be called out. (6.06-a) — A batter is out for illegal action when he hits a ball with one or both feet on the ground entirely outside the batter's box. Rule 6.06-a Comment: If a batter hits a ball fair or foul while out of the batter's box, he shall be called out. Umpires should pay particular attention to the position of the batter's feet if he attempts to hit the ball while he is being intentionally passed. A batter cannot jump or step out of the batter's box and hit the ball.

5. True. Preceding runners are not affected by following runners unless the third out is a forceout or the batter-runner is retired at first base. The appeal at second base was not a forceout. (4.09-a) — One run shall be scored each time a runner legally advances to and touches first, second, third, and home base before three men are put out to end the inning. EXCEPTION: A run is not scored if the runner advances to home base during a play in which the third out is made (1) by the batter-runner before he touches first base; (2) by any runner being forced out; or (3) by a preceding runner who is declared out because he failed to touch one of the bases.

6. True. The runner crossed the plate on a play in which the batter-runner made the third out before he touched first base. (4.09-a). See the rule in question 5.

7. False. The batter is out. This is an Infield Fly. (2.00) — An INFIELD FLY is a fair fly ball (not including a line drive or an attempted bunt) which can be caught by an infielder with ordinary effort, when first and second, or first, second, and third bases are occupied, before two are out. The pitcher, catcher, and any outfielder who stations himself in the infield on the play shall be considered infielders for the purpose of this rule. When it seems apparent that a batted ball will be an Infield Fly, the umpire shall immediately declare "Infield Fly" for the benefit of the runners. If the ball is near the baselines, the umpire shall declare "Infield Fly, if Fair." The ball is alive and runners may advance at the risk of the ball being caught, or retouch and advance after the ball is touched, the same as on any fly ball. If the hit becomes a foul ball, it is treated the same as any foul. If a declared Infield Fly is allowed to fall untouched to the ground, and bounces foul before passing first or third base, it is a foul ball. If a declared Infield Fly falls untouched to the ground outside the baseline, and bounces fair before passing first or third base, it is an Infield Fly.

8. False. See definition of a "Ball." It is a home run. A pitch that bounces can be hit. (2.00) — A ball is a pitch which does not enter the strike zone in flight and is not struck at by the batter. Rule 2.00 (Ball) Comment: If the pitch touches the ground and bounces through the strike zone it is a "ball." If such a pitch touches the batter, he shall be awarded first base. If the batter swings at such a pitch after two strikes, the ball cannot be caught, for the purposes of Rule 6.05-c and 6.09-b. If the batter hits such a pitch, the ensuing action shall be the same as if he hit the ball in flight.

9. False. The batter is safe. To be declared out, a batter must have a foot entirely outside the batter's box. The line is considered part of the box. (6.03) — The batter's legal position shall be with both feet within the batter's box. APPROVED RULING: The lines defining the box are within the batter's box.

10. False. Since Howard did not make a voluntary and intentional release of the ball, it is no catch. (2.00) — A catch is the act of a fielder in getting secure possession in his hand or glove of a ball in flight and firmly holding it. No interference should be allowed when a fielder reaches over a fence, railing, rope, or into a stand to catch a ball. He does so at his own risk.

ANSWERS TO QUIZ 11 *From page 48*

1. Besides Barry Bonds (1993, 2001), the five other San Francisco players to win an N.L. home run title are Orlando Cepeda (1961), Willie Mays (1962, 1964, 1965), Willie McCovey (1963, 1968, 1969), Kevin Mitchell (1989), and Matt Williams (1994).

2. Since 1900, Ichiro Suzuki is the only major league player to record 200 or more singles in one season when he totaled 225 in 2004 and 203 in 2007 with the Mariners. Before 1900, the only player to accomplish the feat was Willie Keeler with 206 in 1898 with Baltimore.

3. Don Sutton is the only 300-game-winning pitcher to post only one 20-victory season during his career, when he went 21-10 in 1976 for the Dodgers.

4. Besides Mel Ott and Willie Mays, the other member of the 500-home run club to hit only seven grand slams during his career was Mike Schmidt.

5. Lou Gehrig holds the major league record for hitting the most home runs in a season against one team when he clubbed 14 of his 49 home runs in 1936 against the Cleveland Indians.

6. Since 1990, the only major league player to combine for 300 or more RBIs in back-to-back seasons is Manny Ramirez, who totaled 310 runs batted in for Cleveland in 1998 (145) and 1999 (165).

7. The two players who tied for the National League Most Valuable Player award in 1979 were first basemen Willie Stargell of the Pittsburgh Pirates and Keith Hernandez of the St. Louis Cardinals.

8. Frank Robinson hit 30 or more home runs in a season with the Cincinnati Reds, Baltimore Orioles, and California Angels during his 21 seasons in the majors. Robinson's career totals were 324 for the Reds, 179 for the Orioles, 19 for the Dodgers, 50 for the Angels, and 14 for the Indians.

9. The seven players to lead the league in stolen bases during their careers while totaling 3,000 lifetime hits are Honus Wagner, Ty Cobb, Eddie Collins, Willie Mays, Lou Brock, Rickey Henderson, and Craig Biggio.

10. Besides Nolan Ryan, the three other pitchers to throw a no-hit game in the major leagues with different teams are Jim Bunning (Tigers and Phillies), Hideo Nomo (Dodgers and Red Sox), and Randy Johnson (Mariners and Diamondbacks).

ANSWERS TO PHOTO QUIZ 3

From page 50

A — Dave Concepcion (5)
B — Willie Mays (12)
C— Julio Franco (8)
D — Rod Carew (3)
E — Casey Stengel (21)
F — Lou Whitaker (23)
G — Ernie Banks (1)
H — Sandy Koufax (11)
I — Joe Torre (22)
J — Derek Jeter (10)

K — Frank Robinson (17)
L — Minnie Minoso (15)
M — Jimmie Foxx (7)
N — Tris Speaker (20)
O — Keith Hernandez (9)
P — Dave Winfield (24)
Q — Will Clark (4)
R — Joe Medwick (14)
S — Nolan Ryan (19)
T — Cal Ripken (16)

ANSWERS TO QUIZ 12   *From page 51*

1. The two players to hit 20 or more doubles, triples, and home runs while stealing 20 or more bases in 2007 were Curtis Granderson of the Tigers and Jimmy Rollins of the Phillies. Granderson hit 38 doubles, 23 triples, and 23 homers with 26 steals for Detroit while Rollins clubbed 38 doubles, 20 triples, and 30 HR with 41 steals for the Phillies.

2. Babe Ruth had the most major league seasons with 40 or more homers with 11.

3. The ten players with 3,000 or more career hits who did not win a batting title in the majors are Paul Molitor, Eddie Collins, Eddie Murray, Cal Ripken, Robin Yount, Dave Winfield, Craig Biggio, Rickey Henderson, Lou Brock, and Rafael Palmeiro.

4. The last major league pitcher to work 300 or more innings in one season was Steve Carlton, who completed 304 innings for the Philadelphia Phillies in 1980.

5. Tom Seaver holds the big league record for pitchers with nine consecutive seasons with 200 or more strikeouts when he accomplished the feat from 1968 through 1976 with the New York Mets.

6. George Brett did not win consecutive batting titles during his career in the major leagues. Brett's three hitting championships were won with the Kansas City Royals in 1976, 1980, and 1990.

7. The two players to hit .400 or higher in a season in the major leagues and not win a batting title were Joe Jackson and Ty Cobb. Jackson hit .408 for the Indians in 1911 and placed second in the A.L. to Cobb's .420 mark with the Tigers. Cobb hit .401 for the Tigers in 1922 but ranked second to George Sisler's .420 BA with the St. Louis Browns.

8. John Tudor posted a 21-8 won-lost record for the Cardinals in 1985 along with ten shutouts and a 1.93 ERA but did not win the N.L. Cy Young Award. The honor was captured by Dwight Gooden of the Mets who went 24-4 with a 1.53 ERA and eight shutouts.

9. The 13 future Hall of Fame pitchers that Hank Aaron hit a home run against during his career were Hoyt Wilhelm, Robin Roberts, Sandy Koufax, Don Drysdale, Juan Marichal, Bob Gibson, Gaylord Perry, Don Sutton, Jim Bunning, Tom Seaver, Ferguson Jenkins, Steve Carlton, and Nolan Ryan.

10. During his career, Lou Gehrig had the most seasons with 150 or more runs batted in: seven — more than any other player in big league history. Gehrig had 175 RBIs in 1927, 174 in 1930, 184 in 1931, 151 in 1932, 165 in 1934, 152 in 1936, and 159 in 1937 with the Yankees.

Puzzle 6 Solution from page 52

```
K E N J I   M A T H E W S O N
I   I   R   A   E   A   T   O
L O C K O U T   R U S S E L L
L   H   N   S   R   T   E   A
E N O S   J U L Y   F R A N
B   L       Z     E   E
R I S E R   A L E X A N D E R
E   I   K   C   R     Y
W I L L C L A R K   M A C H A
    E   K   E     R     N
L E A D   E A R L   C O B B
O   Y   A   N   S   O   S   R
S H E L L E D   L A R U S S A
E   O   O   E   E   T   E   U
R O N G U I D R Y   A N S O N
```

ANSWERS TO QUIZ 13 From page 54

1. The only brothers to win a Cy Young Award are Jim and Gaylord Perry. Jim won the honor in the American League in 1970 with the Minnesota Twins. Gaylord captured the award in the A.L. in 1972 with the Cleveland Indians and in 1978 in the N.L. with the San Diego Padres.

2. Harry and Dixie Walker are the only brothers to win batting titles in the major leagues. Dixie won the N.L. hitting championship in 1944 with the Brooklyn Dodgers and Harry won the N.L. crown in 1947 with the Philadelphia Phillies.

3. Besides Ken and Clete Boyer, the only other brother duo to win Gold Glove awards are Roberto and Sandy Alomar, Jr.

4. The only brothers elected to the Hall of Fame as players are Lloyd and Paul Waner. Paul was inducted in 1952 and Lloyd was honored in 1967.

5. The only father-and-son combination to each steal 50 or more bases in a single season in the major leagues are Maury and Bump Wills. Maury swiped 50-plus bases in 1960, 1962, 1964, and 1965 with the Dodgers and 1968 with the Pirates. Bump accomplished the feat in 1978 with the Texas Rangers.

6. The Alou brothers — Matty, Felipe, and Jesus — played together in the outfield in the same game on September 22, 1963 with the San Francisco Giants against the New York Mets at Candlestick Park.

7. Bob and Ken Forsch are the only brothers to pitch a no-hitter in the major leagues. Ken accomplished the feat on April 7, 1979, for the Houston Astros against the Atlanta Braves. Bob did it for the Cardinals on April 16, 1978, against the Phillies and again on September 26, 1983, vs. the Expos.

8. The brothers who won the most combined games in the major leagues with 539 are Phil and Joe Niekro. Phil finished his career with 318 victories and Joe won 221 games.

9. The only father-and-son combination to win All-Star Game Most Valuable Player awards are Ken Griffey and Ken Griffey, Jr. Junior won the honor in 1992 with the

Seattle Mariners, and his father was voted the trophy in 1980 with the Cincinnati Reds.

10. The only brothers to hit a home run in the same World Series game are Ken and Clete Boyer in Game 7 of the 1964 Fall Classic. Ken hit his for the Cardinals off Yankees' pitcher Steve Hamilton in the seventh inning while Clete of the Yankees connected against Cardinals' ace Bob Gibson in the ninth.

ANSWERS TO
RULES CHALLENGE 6 *From page 55*

1. False. The runner may tag up and advance the moment the ball is touched (Rule 2.00).

2. False. The final score should be 6-5. In this case, the game ends immediately when the winning run scores. (Rule 10.06-f) — Subject to the provisions of Rule 10.06-g, when a batter ends a game with a safe hit that drives in as many runs as are necessary to put his team in the lead, the official scorer shall credit such batter with only as many bases on his hit as are advanced by the runner who scores the winning run, and then only if the batter runs out his hit for as many bases as are advanced by the runner who scores the winning run.

3. False. Upton is out, and because of his interference, no runners may advance. (Rule 7.09-m) — It is interference by a batter or a runner when if, in the judgment of the umpire, a batter-runner willfully and deliberately interferes with a batted ball or a fielder in the act of fielding a batted ball, with the obvious intent to break up a double play. The ball is dead; the umpire shall call the batter-runner out for interference and shall also call out the runner who had advanced closest to the home plate regardless where the double play might have been possible. In no event shall bases be run because of such interference.

4. True. A runner must tag up and start from a contact with the base after the ball is caught. (Rule 7.10-a) — "Retouch," in this rule, means to tag up and start from contact with the base after the ball is caught. A runner is not permitted to take a flying start from a position in back of his base.

5. True. While the ball is alive, runners may retreat after touching the next base. In dead-ball situations, such as a home run, runners may not. (Rule 7.02) — In advancing, a runner shall touch first, second, third, and home base in order. If forced to return, he shall retouch all bases in reverse order.

6. False. Hermida is within his rights to continue to run despite the fact that he was already called out. The onus is on the defense to be aware that Hermida was already called out (7.09-e) —If the batter or a runner continues to advance after he has been put out, he shall not by that act alone be considered as confusing, hindering, or impeding the fielders.

7. True. In domed stadia, a batted ball striking a speaker is in play and can be caught.

8. False. The second trip (by manager or coach) to the same pitcher in the same inning causes that pitcher to be removed from the game. (Rule 8.06-a) — A professional league shall adopt the following rule pertaining to the visit of the manager or coach to the pitcher: (a) This rule limits the number of trips a manager or coach may make to any one pitcher in any one inning; (b) A second trip to the same pitcher in the same inning will cause this pitcher's automatic removal.

9. True. (Rule 2.00) — Obstruction is the act of a fielder who, while not in possession of the ball and not in the act of fielding the ball, impedes the progress of any runner. Rule 2.00 (Obstruction) Comment: If a fielder is about to receive a thrown ball and if the ball is in flight directly toward and near enough to the fielder so he must occupy his position to receive the ball, he may be considered "in the act of fielding a ball." It is entirely up to the judgment of the umpire as to whether a fielder is in the act of fielding a ball.

DID YOU KNOW ... that among the 33 players with 450 or more career home runs, Reggie Jackson is the only member not to have consecutive seasons in which he clubbed 30 or more homers? He smashed 563 lifetime HR with seven seasons of 30-plus homers — but none back-to-back.

10. False. (Rule 9.02-c) — Baserunners must be alert to the possibility that the base umpire on appeal from the plate umpire may reverse the call of a ball to the call of a strike, in which event the runner is in jeopardy of being out by the catcher's throw. Also, a catcher must be alert in a base-stealing situation if a ball call is reversed to a strike by the base umpire upon appeal from the plate umpire. The ball is in play on appeal on a half swing.

ANSWERS TO QUIZ 14 *From page 57*

1. The two shortstops to win 10 or more Gold Glove awards are Ozzie Smith and Omar Vizquel. Smith captured the honor 13 times for the Padres and Cardinals from 1980 through 1992. Vizquel won the award 11 times with the Mariners once (1993), Indians eight times (1994–2001), and Giants twice (2005–2006).

2. Besides Ty Cobb, the only other major league batter to put together two hitting streaks of 30 or more games is George Sisler, who had a 41-game skein in 1922 and a 34-game streak in 1925 for the St. Louis Browns.

3. Besides Darryl Strawberry and Howard Johnson of the Mets, the only other teammates to hit 30 homers and steal 30 bases in the same season are Ellis Burks and Dante Bichette of the Colorado Rockies in 1996.

4. Graig Nettles did not hit 100 or more home runs in both leagues. Among his 390 career homers, 57 were hit in the National League and 333 in the American League.

5. Alfonso Soriano is the only major league player to club 40 or more doubles in a season with four different teams. Soriano hit 51 doubles for the Yankees in 2002, 43 for the Rangers in 2005, 41 for the Nationals in 2006, and 42 for the Cubs in 2007.

6. Tom Seaver never won 20 games in a season for a last-place team. Nolan Ryan won 22 for the last-place Angels in 1974. Roger Clemens won 21 games for the last-place Blue Jays in 1997. Steve Carlton was victorious 27 times for the last-place Phillies in 1972, and Phil Niekro went 21-20 for the last-place Braves in 1979.

7. Tony Cloninger is the only pitcher in major league history to hit two grand slams in one game when he accomplished the feat for the Braves on July 3, 1966, against the San Francisco Giants. In that game, Cloninger went 3-for-5 with nine RBIs — including his two bases-loaded homers.

Jimmie Foxx

8. Besides David Ortiz, the 12 other Red Sox players to win an American League home run title are Buck Freeman (1903), Jake Stahl (1910), Tris Speaker (1912), Babe Ruth (1918–1919), Jimmie Foxx (1939), Ted Williams (1941, 1942, 1947, 1949), Tony Conigliaro (1965), Carl Yastrzemski (1967), Jim Rice (1977–1978, 1983), Dwight Evans (1981), Tony Armas (1984), and Manny Ramirez (2004).

9. The three different league batting champions to wear uniform No. 51 are Willie McGee, Bernie Williams, and Ichiro Suzuki. McGee won the N.L. batting title in 1985 and 1990, Williams the A.L. crown in 1998, and Suzuki captured hitting championships in the A.L. in 2001 and 2004.

10. The three 20-game winners on the 1973 World Series champion Oakland A's were Catfish Hunter (21-5), Vida Blue (20-9), and Ken Holtzman (21-13).

Baseball Fact — When Bob Gibson set a modern major league record with a 1.12 ERA in 1968 he tossed a major league-leading 13 shutouts, including one against every N.L. opponent except the Dodgers. The teams he blanked were the Astros (2), Braves (2), Reds (2), Pirates (2), Phillies (2), Cubs (1), Giants (1), and Mets (1). Gibson also tossed one shutout in the 1968 World Series against the Tigers.